El

by Mark Glaister

All crag photos by Mark Glaister
Other photography as credited
Original ROCKFAX design Alan James and Mick Ryan
Printed by John Browns Printers
Distributed by Cordee (www.cordee.co.uk)

All maps by ROCKFAX

Published by ROCKFAX Ltd. December 2008
© ROCKFAX Ltd. 2008

ISBN 978 1 873341 81 0

www.rockfax.com

Cover: Clare Aspinall on the thin wall climb
No hoy trequa (6a+) - *page 93* - at Escalera Arabe.
Photo: Mike Hutton

Ashley Lewis on the upper section of
Los malos tambien lloran (7a+) - *page 57* - at Túron.
Photo: Chris Sims

Rock Climbing Company

Accommodation - Instruction - Guiding
Performance Coaching - Local Info

- Rock climbing coaching and mountaineering instruction with Silvia Fitzpatrick MIA

- Self-catering accommodation in a typical Spanish mountain village

- Ideally situated between Málaga and Granada

- Close to Archidona, Loja, Cauche, Antequera, Turon and El Chorro

- All levels and different styles of climbing; sport, trad, single and multipitch climbing plus plenty of bouldering and scrambling

- Excellent mountain biking locally and skiing in Sierra Nevada

- Partner, transport and gear provision so that you can just turn up with your shoes and get a lot of climbing done.

- Spanish tuition. Silvia is a native Spanish speaker and a qualified modern languages teacher

- Flexible arrangements to suit your needs

www.rockclimbingcompany.co.uk
silvia@rockclimbingcompany.co.uk
· UK: 0044 (0)1492 641430
Spain: 0034 690105915

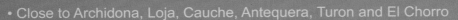

Contents

Introduction 4
   Introducción 10
   Einleitung 12
   Acknowledgements 14
   Advertiser Directory 16
El Chorro Logistics 18
   General Information 20
   Accommodation 28
El Chorro Climbing............. 30
   Gear................................. 32
   Grades 33
   Other Guidebooks 36
   Top 50............................... 38
   Crag Table 42

Mijas 44
Túron 52
El Chorro 62
   Frontales 62
   Escalera Arabe 82
   Las Encantadas 96
   The Gorge 104
   Los Cotos.......................... 120
   El Polvorin 130
   Makinodromo 136
Desplomilandia................ 148
Valle de Abdalajis.............. 162
El Torcal 170
Villanueva de Cauche 180
Archidona 184
Loja 188

Index and Area Map 200

Mijas | Turon | Frontales | Escalera Arabe | Encantadas | The Gorge | Los Cotos | El Polvorin | Makinodromo | Desplomilandia | Abdalajis | El Torcal | V. de Cauche | Archidona | Loja

Paul Cox moving up the final arete of *Pacharan con endrinas* (6c) - page 176 - at Sector La Bodega, El Torcal. Photo: Mark Glaister

Mijas

Turon

Frontales

Escalera Arabe

Encantadas

The Gorge

Los Cotos

El Polvorin

Makinodromo

Desplomilandia

Abdalajis

El Torcal

V. de Cauche

Archidona

Loja

Claire Aspinal on *Steady Away* (6b+) - *page 94* - at Escalera Arabe. Photo: Mike Hutton

The Gorge at El Chorro is a huge limestone defile that slices through the mountain range just 50km inland from the city of Málaga, in the province of Andalucia. This striking landmark is one of the World's most famous sport climbing destinations and was one of the first areas in Europe to be equipped during the development of this style of rock climbing during the 1980's. Since then development has spread to all the surrounding cliffs and walls resulting in a superb set of varied routes from long multi-pitch big wall climbs, to easily-accessed single-pitch sectors. Beyond the confines of The Gorge and its neighbouring cliffs the Andalucian landscape provides limestone aplenty and crags the equal of the best on offer around El Chorro. These fine near neighbours are covered in this Rockfax and are all easily accessed from an El Chorro base for daily visits.

The style of climbing in the area, and the grade range of the 1000 or so climbs described will satisfy all who are planning a visit; ranging from world class hard routes, through a vast selection of superb mid-grade pitches, to an ever-increasing number of sectors and whole crags that give those operating in the easier grades something to go at.

Complementing the climbing is the region itself; its coastal fringe is heavily developed for tourism but the inland mountains are a total contrast, dotted with classic Andalucian villages that cling to the sides, or perch on the summits, of the hills that rise up into the centre of the range. The small towns and villages themselves are excellent places to soak up some of the area's relaxed culture and eat at the seemingly limitless number of tapas bars, whereas the cities of Sevilla and Granada offer an opportunity to sample Spanish city life at its grandest. El Chorro's reputation for top notch sport climbing, stunning countryside and its near-perfect 'off season' climbing weather make it an ideal destination for a first-time winter-sun seeker, or long-term visitor returning looking for something new to do, and bask again in the undoubted charm of this lovely part of the world.

Mijas

Turon

Frontales

Escalera Arabe

Encantadas

The Gorge

Los Cotos

El Polvorin

Makinodromo

Desplomilandia

Abdalajis

El Torcal

V. de Cauche

Archidona

Loja

Neil Binns on the start of the powerful *Tinto con Limón* (7a+) -
page 176 - at Sector La Bodega, El Torcal. Photo: Chris Sims

Mijas

Turon

Frontales

Escalera Arabe

Encantadas

The Gorge

Los Cotos

El Polvorin

Makinodromo

Desplomilandia

Abdalajis

El Torcal

V. de Cauche

Archidona

Loja

The Guidebook History

Rockfax has been producing information for El Chorro since as long ago as 1993 when we published a set of yellow topo cards. After that it took third billing in three editions of the popular *Costa Blanca, Mallorca, El Chorro* guidebook which spanned 1996 to 2004. Since then we have published books to both the Costa Blanca and Mallorca, but El Chorro has had to be content with an online PDF of the 2001 edition of the triple-area guide.

This book brings together all the previous information and adds a lot more in the shape of some stunning full-page photographs for topos, plenty of inspiring action shots, plus a host of new routes and crags across the region. It could almost be said that, after 15 years, we have finally produced a guidebook worthy of this fantastic area!

Route Names

In all the previous Rockfax guidebooks to El Chorro there have been some routes that have never had names. In this edition we have taken the liberty of giving most of the routes names to aid in identification. This is especially useful for those who wish to use the online route databases to give us feedback. In most cases the new names are simply descriptive and are hopefully inoffensive. If you know alternative names for these routes then please let us know using the route databases and we will up date future editions.

The Photography

The photography in this guide is mostly from images captured on compact or SLR digital cameras. The revolution in digital photography has made the compilation and selection of images far easier than in the past. It has also widened the availability of some superb action shots via either personal submissions, or searches on excellent web sites like **www.ukclimbing.com**. As a climbing photographer, I often get asked how people can go about getting the best possible shots? My answer is always the same and doesn't relate to the quality of the camera equipment. I tell people to get themselves out there and make the effort to take the picture even if it might not appear to be from the best angle, or in optimum light conditions. These days the ability to take hundreds of shots at little cost has changed how I work and I now try and take at least one shot on nearly all the climbs I do, or see someone else doing. The results are often quite surprising and occasionally you capture something that you would have missed otherwise.

Mijas

Turon

Frontales

Escalera Arabe

Encantadas

The Gorge

Los Cotos

El Polvorin

Makinodromo

Desplomilandia

Andalajis

El Torcal

V. de Cauche

Archidona

Loja

Starting up *Generacion spontanea* (6c) - *page 134* - at the superb venue of El Polvorin at El Chorro. Photo: Chris Dainton

Mijas

Turon

Frontales

Escalera Arabe

Encantadas

The Gorge

Los Cotos

El Polvorin

Makinodromo

Desplomilandia

Abdalajis

El Torcal

V. de Cauche

Archidona

Loja

Access

Over the years El Chorro has had a number of access problems affecting different crags. Currently the situation is much more stable than it used to be but there are still four areas of concern that the visiting climber needs to be aware of.

1) Railway Tunnels - Access to the railway tunnels is now totally banned with large sections of fencing erected and guards being posted at the entrance to one of the tunnels at popular times. The policing of the tunnels is for safety reasons, due in part to incidents involving people pushing prams through them or walking on the tracks with their iPods on! Although this has made access to the climbing in the Central Gorge area a bit trickier all the crags can still be reached at all times - see page 108.

2) Upper Gorge - Climbing in the Upper Gorge is now banned for environmental reasons and the area has been left out of this book.

3) Wild Camping - No camping or open fires in the National Park.

4) The Walkway - The 'Camino del Rey' itself has had its initial section dismantled but this is now easily bypassed by a via ferrata that starts down the slope from the bridge (see page 108) that is specifically intended for climbers to access The Gorge and avoid using the tunnels. For those who wish to negotiate the whole of the Camino del Rey, including the Upper Gorge, a rope and quickdraws are necessary to negotiate a section that is missing. This section is at the top of the Upper Gorge and necessitates a climb up, across and back down onto the Walkway and has some bolts for protection. This section can't be negotiated by those without climbing experience.

Feedback - El Chorro Route Database

The database at www.rockfax.com contains a listing of every route in the book with the opportunity for you to lodge comments and vote on grades and star ratings. This information is essential to help us ensure complete and up-to-date coverage for all the climbs. We can then produce updates and make sure we get it right in subsequent editions. To make this system work we need the help of everyone who climbs in El Chorro, so if you think you have found a badly graded route, or discovered a hidden gem that we have only given a single star to, let us know about it. Your general comments on all other aspects of this book are also welcome.

Andalucian countryside. Photo: Chris Dainton

Makinodromo

Desplomilandia

Abdalajís

El Torcal

V. de Cauche

Archidona

Loja

Rob Knight on the first section of *Salida de emergencia* (6c) - *page 146* - on
the Life is Sweet Wall at Makinodromo, El Chorro. Photo: Mark Glaister

El Chorro es uno de los mejores lugares en Europa para la escalada. Este cañon impressionante y su espectacular roca de los alrededores fue unos de las primeras escuelas desarroladas en España cuando la escalada deportiva empezó en la década de los ochenta. Tiene todo lo que el escalador nómada puede pedir - vias fantásticas, precios baratos, muchas opciones de alojamiento y, lo más importante, buen tiempo durante los meses de invierno. El famoso cañon y su sendero espectacular (El Camino del Rey) ofrecen una escalada única, aunque actualmente hay más sectores abiertos en la area que están llenos de vias de excelente calidad y de todos los grados.

Acceso

La mayoría de vias en este libro no tienen problemas de acceso y se pueden escalar todo el tiempo. Los túneles del tren que están usados para acceder algunos sectores en el cañon y más allá han sido cerrados a peatones por razones de seguridad. Por esta razón las aproximaciones a los sectores son un poco más dificiles aunque aún es possible usar el sendero que pasa por encima de los túneles, o usando el sendero que atraviesa el cañon. Ver la página 108 para más información.

La guía

Esta guía de escalada contiene la información necesaria para localizar y evaluar las mejores escaladas en la isla aunque tu idioma no sea el inglés. Los mapas te van a ayudar a llegar a los sectores y las reseñas y símbolos te van a mostrar que vias hay en el sector.

Material

La mayoria de las vías deportivas en esta guía estan bien equipadas por las cuales sólo se necesita un juego de cintas exprés y una cuerda larga. Recomendamos el uso de cuerdas de almenos 60 metros. Si quieres escalar vías de varios largos vas a necesitar cuerdas dobles de 9 milímetros y 50 metros para los rápeles.

Internet

Todas la vías de esta guía estan incluidas en el "Rockfax Route Database" del Rockfax sitio web - **www.rockfax.com**. Allí puedes encontrar más información sobre las vías como la votación de grados y comentarios de otros escaladores. Si no estas de acuerdo con los grados de las vías que has escalado, entra en el "Rockfax Route Database" y dinos lo que piensas.

Rockfax

Rockfax ha estado produciendo guías de escalada desde 1990. Estas son 27 guías de escuelas europeas y 4 guías de escuelas en Estado Unidos. También hemos producido más de 50 miniguías en formato PDF que puedes encontrar en nuestro sitio web. Recientemente hemos publicado una serie de manuales de entrenamiento de escalada. Más información en **www.rockfax.com**

Mijas

Turon

Frontales

Escalera Arabe

Encantadas

The Gorge

Los Cotos

El Polvorin

Makinodromo

Desplomilandia

Abdalajis

El Torcal

V. de Cauche

Archidona

Loja

Símbolos de las vías

 Vía buena que mereze ser escalada.

 Vía muy buena, una de las mejores del sector.

 Vía excelente, una de las mejores en la región.

 Una de las 50 vías más populares del libro. Ver página 38.

 Escalada técnica que requiere buen equlibrio y técnica, o pasos difíciles y delicados.

 Escalada de fuerza; techos, desplomes o pasos de presas pequeñas que alejan.

 Escalada de continuidad; muchos pasos duros o roca desplomada que hace la escalada agotadora.

 Escalada de regleta con presas pequeñas en los pasos difíciles.

 Escalada delicada con peligro de caída y seguros que alejan.

 Es necesario hacer pasos largos o que alejan en una o varias partes de la vía.

 Vía semi-equipada. Es necesario llevar un juego de fisureros y friends.

 Se puede encontrar roca descompuesta en la vía.

Símbolos de las paredes

 Inclinación del sendero con el tiempo estimado de aproximación.

 Tiempo del día cuando le da el sol al sector (en dias soleados).

 Se puede escalar en caso de lluvia.

 La roca puede tener filtraciones de agua después de períodos de lluvia.

 Sector de escalada expuesto, puede hacer frío cuando sopla el viento. Possiblemente en media/alta montaña

 Sector protegido del viento.

 Desierto - Sector en desuso y normalmente sin gente. La aproximación puede ser larga y/o con vías de poca calidad.

 Tranquilo - Partes mas tranquilas de los sectores, o buenos sectores con aproximación larga.

 Concurrido - Sectores donde raramente vas a estar sólo, especialmente en los fines de semana. Vías buenas.

 Multitud - Los sectores más populares que siempre están llenos de gente.

Código de color de los grados

Todas las vías de escalada tienen un código de color que indica a que banda de grado corresponden:

1 4+ o menos

2 5 a 6a+

3 6b a 7a

4 7a+ o más

Reunión equipada — **A** — Punto de rápel
Descuelgue
Alternativa para la misma vía
7
6
5
4
3

Edificios
Pueblo
Pista sin asfaltar
A-9270
Aparcamiento **P**
Pared(es) de escalada
A92
Camping
Escala
N

Mijas · Turón · Frontales · Escalera Arabe · Encantadas · The Gorge · Los Cotos · El Polvorín · Makinodromo · Desplomilandia · Abdalajís · El Torcal · V. de Cauche · Archidona · Loja

El Chorro ist eines der bekanntesten Kletterziele in Europa. Diese dramatische Schlucht, sowie die spektakulären Felsen der Umgebung war eines der ersten Gebiete in Spanien, die entwickelt wurden als Sportklettern in den 1980er Jahren begann. Das Gebiet hat alles, was anreisende Kletterer von einem qualitativ hochwertigen Wintersonnen Kletterziel erwarten: großartige Routen, preiswerte Anreise, reichlich Unterkünfte und vor allem gutes Wetter während der kälteren Wintermonate.

Die berühmte Schlucht und ihr spektakulärer "Wehrgang" (der El Camino del Rey) offerieren eine einzigartige Klettererfahrung. Heutzutage sind in diesem Gebiet wesentlich mehr Felsen verfügbar, die meist Weltklassekletterein im gesamten Schwierigkeitsbereich bieten.

Zugang

Die Mehrzahl der Routen in diesem Kletterführer sind problemlos zugänglich und können jederzeit geklettert werden. Die Eisenbahntunnel, die als Zugang zu einigen Felsen in und um die Schlucht von El Choro dienten, sind aus Sicherheitsgründen für Wanderer geschlossen worden. Das hat den Zugang zu einigen Felsen etwas schwieriger gemacht. Gleichwohl ist ein Zugang möglich, wenn man einen neuen Pfad über die Tunnel oder den "Wehrgang" durch die Schlucht benutzt. Siehe Seite 108 für weitere Informationen.

Der Kletterführer

Dieses Buch enthält sämtliche Informationen die Du benötigst, um die besten Felsen des Gebietes aufzufinden und einzuschätzen - auch wenn Englisch nicht Deine Muttersprache ist. Topos und Symbole veranschaulichen die Art von Routen, die Dich an Deinem Ziel erwarten.

Ausrüstung

Die meisten Routen in diesem Kletterführer sind voll ausgerüstete Sportkletterrouten, für die lediglich ein Satz Expreßschlingen und ein langes Seil benötigt wird. Ein 60 Meter Seil ist angebracht, um sicher abseilen zu können. Wenn Du beabsichtigst, einige der Mehrseillängenrouten zu klettern, sind 9mm Doppelseile mit 50 Meter Länge fürs Abseilen unumgänglich.

Internet

Alle beschriebenen Aufstiege dieses Kletterführers sind in der Rockfax Routendatenbank auf der Internetseite - www.rockfax.com - enthalten. Hier findest Du auch mehr Informationen über die einzelnen Routen, einschließlich Votings zu Schwierigkeitseinstufungen und Kommentare anderer Kletterer. Wenn Du Routen kletterst und nicht mit diesem Kletterführer übereinstimmst, dann besuche unsere Datenbank, um uns Deine Meinung mitzuteilen.

Rockfax

Rockfax veröffentlicht seit 1990 Kletterführer. Das schließt 27 Bücher zu Gebieten in Europa und 4 Bücher zu Gebieten in den USA ein. Darüber hinaus sind auf der Rockfax Website mehr als 50 Miniguides im PDF-Format verfügbar. In letzter Zeit haben wir eine Serie von Büchern zum Thema Leistungstraining veröffentlicht. Weitere Informationen findest Du auf unserer Internetseite - **www.rockfax.com**

Mijas
Turon
Frontales
Escalera Arabe
Encantadas
The Gorge
Los Cotos
El Polvorin
Makinodromo
Desplomilandia
Abdalajis
El Torcal
V. de Gaucin
Archidona
Inia

Symbole

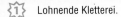 Lohnende Kletterei.

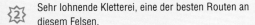 Sehr lohnende Kletterei, eine der besten Routen an diesem Felsen.

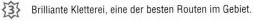 Brilliante Kletterei, eine der besten Routen im Gebiet.

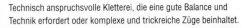 Eine der populärsten Routen in diesem Buch, Bestandteil der "Top 50" (siehe Seite 38).

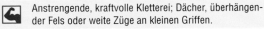 Technisch anspruchsvolle Kletterei, die eine gute Balance und Technik erfordert oder komplexe und trickreiche Züge beinhaltet.

 Anstrengende, kraftvolle Kletterei; Dächer, überhängender Fels oder weite Züge an kleinen Griffen.

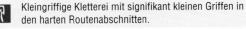 Durchweg anstrengende Kletterei; entweder mit vielen harten Zügen oder überhängender Fels, der zu dicken Armen führt.

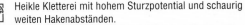 Kleingriffige Kletterei mit signifikant kleinen Griffen in den harten Routenabschnitten.

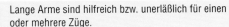 Heikle Kletterei mit hohem Sturzpotential und schaurig weiten Hakenabständen.

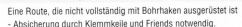 Lange Arme sind hilfreich bzw. unerläßlich für einen oder mehrere Züge.

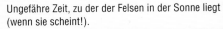 Eine Route, die nicht vollständig mit Bohrhaken ausgerüstet ist - Absicherung durch Klemmkeile und Friends notwendig.

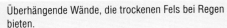 Möglicherweise lockerer Fels im Routenverlauf.

Felsymbole

 Steilheit des Zugangsweges mit ungefährer Zeitangabe.

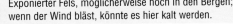 Ungefähre Zeit, zu der der Felsen in der Sonne liegt (wenn sie scheint!).

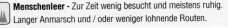 Überhängende Wände, die trockenen Fels bei Regen bieten.

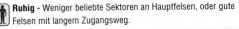 Rinnwasser, der Fels tropft nach längerem Regen.

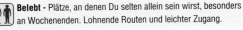 Exponierter Fels, möglicherweise hoch in den Bergen; wenn der Wind bläst, könnte es hier kalt werden.

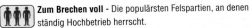 Windgeschützter bzw. warmer Fels.

Menschenleer - Zur Zeit wenig besucht und meistens ruhig. Langer Anmarsch und / oder weniger lohnende Routen.

Ruhig - Weniger beliebte Sektoren an Hauptfelsen, oder gute Felsen mit langem Zugangsweg.

Belebt - Plätze, an denen Du selten allein sein wirst, besonders an Wochenenden. Lohnende Routen und leichter Zugang.

Zum Brechen voll - Die populärsten Felspartien, an denen ständig Hochbetrieb herrscht.

Farbig markierte Routennummern

Die farbigen Routennummern entsprechen den folgenden Schwierigkeitsbereichen:

1 Grad V+ und darunter

2 Grad VI- bis VII-

3 Grad VII bis VIII

4 Grad VIII+ und darüber

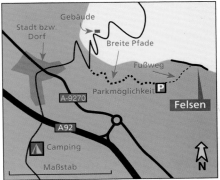

Seitenregister (rechter Rand): Mijas · Túron · Frontales · Escalera Arabe · Encantadas · The Gorge · Los Cotos · El Polvorín · Makinodromo · Desplomilandia · Abdalajís · El Torcal · V. de Cauche · Archidona · Loja

Over the past 15 years my trips to El Chorro and its neighbouring crags have left me with some of the best memories of my climbing life, both on and off the rock. Stunning climbs, fine countryside, lots of fun times and great company have all intermingled and left me a little lost when it comes to planning on going somewhere else. Many thanks to all those who I have shared a rope with, helped with the guidebook and of course to those who have grafted hard to put up the routes for us all to enjoy.

Thanks especially to Lee Proctor, Paul Cox, Dave Henderson, Marti Hallett, Arran Deakin, Rob Knight, Alison Martindale, Phil Black, Chris Gore, Jon Hofor, Rob Sutton, Ken Palmer, Steve Watt, Clare Dyson, Natalie Prensa, Duncan Booth, Rich Harris, Rich and Sam Mayfield, Wilf and Jane Williamson, Emma Medara, Gav, Caff, Hock, Wes and Alan and Helen at Finca Los Llanos.

The photography in this book has been supplemented with some stunning contributions from Mike Hutton, Chris Dainton, Dave Pickford, and Chris Sims.

Thanks also to Chris Craggs, Sherri Davy, Martin Heywood, Hillary Lawrenson, Keith Waddell, Karsten Kurz, Ramon Marin and André Selmer for their help with translations, checking, advertising and last minute information.

As ever we are very grateful to all those who have contributed to the documentation of information in the area. The bulk of the work in the earlier Rockfax editions was undertaken by Mike Owen and Rab Anderson, which was based in part on Chris Craggs' Andalucia Rock Climbs (1992). Other local guides have been produced by Pedro Garcia, Juan Carlos Perez, Javier Romero Rubiols and David Munilla.

Thanks also to Alan who as usual has been brilliant to work with and together this year we also managed a first - a holiday where it didn't rain, in Lofoten of all places!

Once again a huge thanks to Rachel for her support and patience and to my constant office companions Jack, George and Harvey.

Mark Glaister, in El Chorro, November 2008

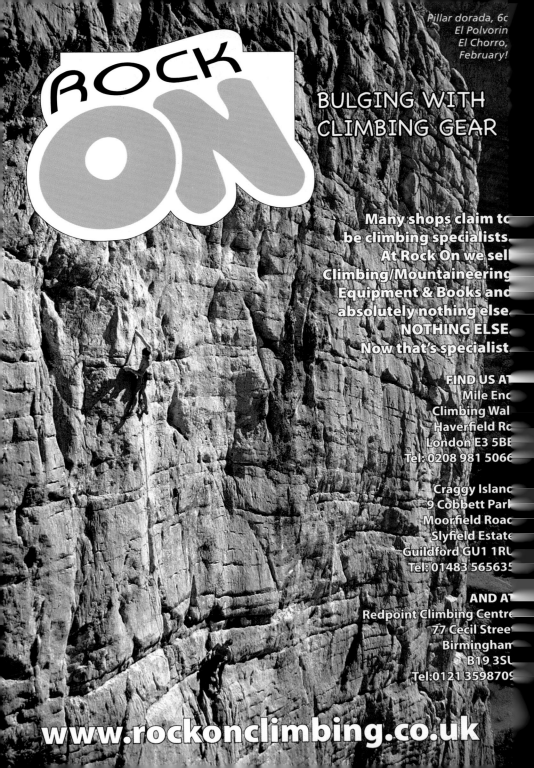

Rockfax is grateful to the following companies who have supported this guidebook.

Accommodation and Guiding

Finca La Campana - Inside back cover
Tel: +34 626963942
www.el-chorro.com

The Rock Climbing Company - Page 2
Tel: (UK) 0044 (0)1492 641430
Tel: (Spain) 0034 690105915
www.rockclimbingcompany.co.uk

Accommodation

Ardales Village - Page 21
Tel: +34 635105943
www.ardalesvillage.com

Finca Rocabella - Page 23
www.fincarocabella.com

La Almona Chica - Page 29
www.holiday-rentals.com (number 2678)

Finca Los Llanos - Page 27
Tel: +34 686 291 485
www.fincalosllanos.com

Fuego Blanco - Page 29
Tel: +34 952497439
www.fuegoblanco.com

El Arpa - Page 23
Tel: +34 645 643 108
www.FincaMalaga.com

Gear Shops

Rock On - Page 15
Mile End and Craggy Island - in London
Redpoint, Birmingham
Tel: (ME) 0208 981 5066 (CI) 01483 565635
(RP) 0121 3598709
www.rockonclimbing.co.uk

Climbing Walls

Awesome Walls - Page 25
St. Alban's Church, Athol Street, Liverpool.
Tel/Fax: 0151 298 2422
The Engine House, Stockport.
Tel: 0161 494 9949
www.awesomewalls.co.uk

Outdoor Gear

Berghaus - Inside front cover
Extreme Centre, Sunderland.
Tel: 0191 516 5600
www.berghaus.com

Black Diamond - Outside back cover
Tel: 0162 958 0484
www.blackdiamondequipment.com

Climbers' Web Resource

Climb Europe - Page 27
www.climb-europe.com

The beautiful lakes above El Chorro
passed on the way to the crags of
Desplomilandia. Photo: Mark Glaister

Mijas · Turon · Frontales · Escalera Arabe · Encantadas · The Gorge · Los Cotos · El Polvorin · Makinodromo · Desplomilandia · Abdalajis · El Torcal · V. de Cauche · Archidona · Loja

Mijas

Turón

Frontales

Escalera Árabe

Encantadas

The Gorge

Los Cotos

El Polvorín

Makinodromo

Desplomilandia

Abdalajis

El Torcal

V. de Cauche

Archidona

Loja

The sustained line of *Heat Exchange* (6c+) - *page 147* - at
the deceptively steep Mega Flash area of Makinodromo,
El Chorro. Climber: Paul Cox. Photo: Mark Glaister

Mijas

Tiron

Frontales

Escalera Arabe

Encantadas

The Gorge

Los Cotos

El Polvorín

Makinodromo

Desplomilandia

Abdalajis

El Torcal

V. de Cauche

Archidona

Loja

El Chorro Logistics

Photo: Dave Pickford

Mijas | Turon | Frontales | Escalera Arabe | Encantadas | The Gorge | Los Cotos | El Polvorin | Makinodromo | Desplomilandia | Abdalajis | El Torcal | V. de Gauche | Archidona | Loja

The Walkway (or Camino del Rey) provides a unique and atmospheric way to access many of the climbs in The Gorge at El Chorro. Photo: Chris Dainton

Flights

The main airport for the area is Málaga International Airport. Luckily this is one of the best served and most popular airports in Europe and with flights from all major European destinations all year round. Prices are some of the cheapest available to any climbing destination in Spain and look likely to stay that way for the foreseeable future. If a bit of time is spent searching out the bargains outside of the holiday periods, it is still not uncommon to be able to pick up return flights from the UK for £65 or less.

www.easyjet.com - from East Midlands, Bristol, Glasgow, Liverpool, London Airports, Manchester, Newcastle.

www.bmibaby.com - from Birmingham, Cardiff ,East Midlands, Manchester.

www.flybe.com - from Exeter, Southampton.

www.jet2.com - from Belfast, Newcastle, Blackpool, Manchester, Leeds/Bradford.

www.ryanair.com - from Stansted, Birmingham, Bournemouth, East Midlands, Edinburgh, Glasgow, Liverpool.

It is also worth checking on charter flight availability as occasionally they are cheaper, especially for trips during holiday periods.

www.cheap-flights.com, **www.charterflights.co.uk**.

Car Hire

El Chorro is perhaps the best of Spain's major winter sun climbing destinations to consider for those wishing not to hire a car, but having one makes getting to other nearby spots possible and is essential for those who don't like walking very much! Car hire is relatively cheap - in the region of €15/day for a small car. All the following companies have on-airport offices and pick-up and drop-off. **www.holidayautos.co.uk**, **www.europcar.com**, **www.hertz.com**

Without a Car

El Chorro, more than any of the other winter sun climbing destinations in Europe, lends itself to those on a tight budget, or those who wish to climb without making use of a car. Travel from Málaga's airport or train station to Alora, and then on to El Chorro, is relatively straightforward and cheap. From the accommodation centred on El Chorro it is possible to walk to many of the areas great cliffs such as Encantadas, Makinodromo, The Gorge and Frontales. For the crags further afield, hitching a lift is a real possibility, or hooking up with others with transport in the cafe, bar or refugio. The small food shops in El Chorro stock all the basics.

Mijas | Turon | Frontales | Escalera Arabe | Encantadas | The Gorge | Los Cotos | El Polvorin | Makinodromo | Desplomilandia | Abdalajis | El Torcal | V. de Cauche | Archidona | Loja

Getting Around

The road network in and around Málaga is good and the approach to El Chorro and a number of the other crags has improved greatly since the last Rockfax was published in 2001. Road signs and road numbers still seem to be a little random at times and missing a junction or a turn-off is common on the 'onsight' approach to some of the crags. Speed traps and cameras are on the increase and on-the-spot fines are common. A few of the crags require that the final approach be made on dirt tracks; none of the tracks are too bad but care should be taken as the drop-offs on some of them are impressive!
See the area map on page 200.

Public Transport

There are good public transport links from Málaga Airport to the town Alora, south of El Chorro. The train service to El Chorro itself is in a state of flux and the train times seem to change regularly so it is best to check before travelling (952 360 202). The railway service to Alora is good and from Alora it is easy to catch a taxi or hitch a lift to El Chorro. The number for taxis in Alora is 952 496 424.

There is a bus service but it is probably best to check locally on the routes and times at the tourist information office in Alora (952 495 577).

Mountain goats and
The Gorge at El Chorro.
Photo: Chris Painter

Weather

The best weather for climbing is normally to be found between the middle of October and the beginning of May. During this period the air temperatures can be perfect and the options of sun, shade and/or altitude can be utilised to keep the ambient temperature comfortable. It can be cold so a warm coat and hat are advisable additions to the packing list. However it is more likely to be on the warm side so shorts, suncream and a sunhat should also not be forgotten. Wet weather does occasionally close in but the chances of a complete wash out are low and there is usually always somewhere dry to climb. Summer is most definitely not the time to be planning on a trip, as inland temperatures regularly hit 40°C, although high up in the shade at Loja or El Torcal it might be cool enough to venture out on to the rock without frying.

Temperature °C	Jan	Feb	Mar	Apr	May	Jun	Jul	Aug	Sep	Oct	Nov	Dec
Maximum (average)	16	17	18	20	23	25	30	35	29	23	19	17
Minimum (average)	10	11	12	13	15	18	20	22	19	17	14	11

Rainfall Days	Jan	Feb	Mar	Apr	May	Jun	Jul	Aug	Sep	Oct	Nov	Dec
Average per month	7	6	6	6	4	3	2	1	3	7	6	6

Public Holidays

It is well worth taking note of the Spanish public holidays as most of the shops, bars and cafes are closed on these days and public transport will be limited.
1st January (New Year), 6th January (Epiphany), 28th February (Andalucia Day),
March/April (Easter Thursday and Good Friday), 1st May (Labour Day),
15th August (Assumption), 12th October (National Day), 1st November (All Saints' Day),
6th December (Spanish Constitution Day), 8th December (The Immaculate Conception),
25th December (Christmas Day).

Photo: Chris Dainton

Mijas · Turon · Frontales · Escalera Arabe · Encantadas · The Gorge · Los Cotos · El Polvorin · Makinodromo · Desplomilandia · Abdalajis · El Torcal · V. de Cauche · Archidona · Loja

> ## Mountain Rescue
> **Dial 112** - Ensure you have details of your location and what the incident involves. This number works on any mobile on a Spanish network.

Travel Insurance
Although also part of the EU and subject to providing medical help for other EU residents under the EHIC (European Health Insurance Card) scheme it is strongly recommended that personal travel insurance is taken out to cover rescue, medical and repatriation following an accident. **BMC Travel Insurance** - **www.thebmc.com**

Shops and Eating Out
For the El Chorro based visitor there are a number of small shops spread out around the village that stock all that is needed to sustain a visit. Meals are served at the Refugio, the Station Bar and the La Garganta Hotel. Further afield there are many more options. Alora is around 10km from El Chorro and has lots of bars, restaurants, cafes and larger supermarkets. Up at the lakes above El Chorro are some superb bars and restaurants that have wonderful views. Málaga (about an hour from El Chorro) has all the attractions, and distractions, of a large city along with hypermarkets on its outskirts.

Climbing Shops
There is a small climbing shop in the centre of El Chorro village that stocks plenty of gear and clothing. Málaga has larger shops.

Other Activities

The climbing shop in El Chorro. Photo: Mark Glaister

For the sunlover the warm Mediterranean waters and sandy beaches are only an hour away. Walkers and mountain bikers will find the hills and mountains of the El Chorro and El Torcal Natural Parks provide plenty of potential. Day visits to the major historic cities of Antequera, Cordoba, Sevilla and Granada are possible by car, or train, from Málaga. There are many opportunities for relaxing in the quiet villages that dot the neighbouring landscape and the city life of Málaga is only a quick train or car journey away. Slightly further afield, but good for a rest day, are the tourist hot-spot of Mijas, a pretty village perched high above the Mediterranean, and the impressive town of Ronda.

A Load of Bull
....and if all else fails you can search this book for the hidden bulls. There are 20 to find, including the one on this page. They are all well hidden in the photos so look closely and log your progress using our bull-ometer below.

Bull	1	2	3	4	5	6	7	8	9	10	11	12	13	14	15	16	17	18	19	20
Page		26																		

Bull-ometer

FINCA LOS LLANOS
CASA LOS OLIVOS

After a good day climbing you deserve some comfort!
Located between the white hill town of Álora and the crags of El Chorro,
we are just a short drive between the best climbing areas
and a good choice of tapas bars and restaurants.

Self Catering or Bed and Breakfast - ideal for couples or groups of up to 10.
Spacious and comfortable accommodation - great breakfasts - friendly hospitality - Wifi Internet.
Car and bike hire, horse riding, tickets and tours, all can be arranged.

Tel: 0034 952495592   Mob: 0034 686 291 485
E-mail fincalosllanos@yahoo.co.uk
Finca Los Llanos, Crtra El Chorro, Km 3, Álora 29500, Málaga, Spain
www.fincalosllanos.com

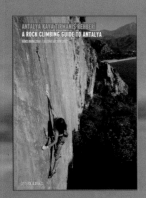

Mijas
Turon
Frontales
Escalera Arabe
Encantadas
The Gorge
Los Cotos
El Polvorin
Makinodromo
Despomilandia
Abdalajis
El Torcal
V. de Cauche
Archidona
Loja

Apartments, Villas and Cottages

There are lots of options available in the immediate surrounds of El Chorro that vary from small cottage-style terraces to huge villas complete with pools and luxury accommodation. There is plenty of accommodation within walking distance of the crags, and the bars at the refugio and station, for those without a car. The surrounding villages and towns also have many places of all shapes and sizes to rent and will be of interest to those looking for a broader selection of shops, eating and cafe/bar options such as those in the bustling town of Alora. The cost of the accommodation is on the best side of reasonable and varies from around €50 to €140 per person, per week.

Web sites worth checking:

www.fuegoblanco.com
www.el-chorro.com
www.holiday-rentals.co.uk (no. 2678)
www.rockclimbingcompany.co.uk
www.fincarocabella.com
www.fincamalaga.com
www.fincarocabella.com
www.fincalosllanos.com
www.ardalesvillage.com

Refuges

There is a refugio in the centre of El Chorro that has very basic accommodation (and a bar) at around €10 per person, per night with breakfast. There are a couple of other excellent refugio-style set-ups in El Chorro village that offer a good standard of accommodation and are fully geared towards the rock climbing market. A big advantage for those travelling on their own is that during the climbing season there are always plenty of other climbers staying at the refugios. There are also refugios in other towns such as Archidona.

Camping

The El Chorro campsite is very close to the climbing and the centre of El Chorro but is not a particularly cheap option with prices of about €10 per person, per night. There are also some small chalets on the campsite that are reasonably priced if the other accommodation locally is full. The website for the camping is **www.alberguecampingelchorro.com**
There are several beautiful campsites up on the shores of the lakes just above El Chorro but these are only open from Easter until the end of September.

Important - Wild camping in the National Park of El Chorro is banned and campfires are also forbidden.

Turon

Frontales

Escalera Arabe

Encantadas

The Gorge

Los Cotos

El Polvorin

Makinodromo

Desplomlandia

Abdalajis

El Torcal

V. de Cauche

Archidona

Loja

Evening sunlight picks out the tufa drapes of El Chorro's most famous section of cliff - Makinodromo, whilst a climber nears the top of *Porrot* (7c+) - *page 145*. Photo: Mark Glaister

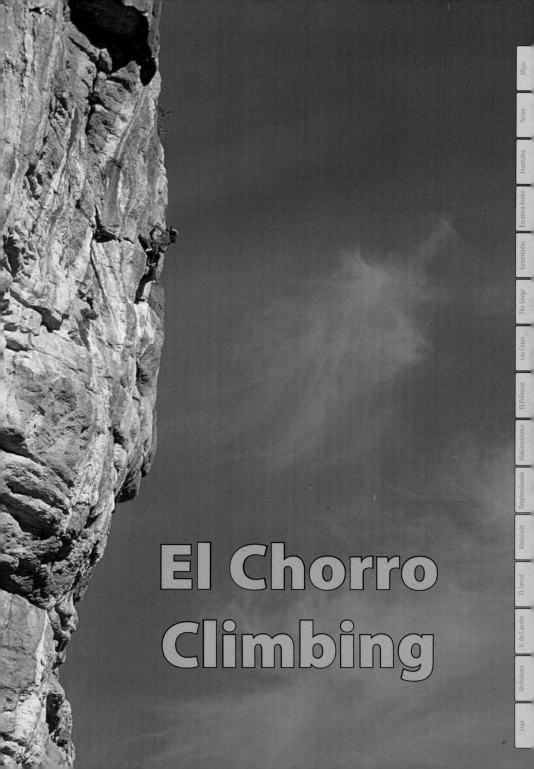

El Chorro
Climbing

Mijas

Túron

Frontales

Escalera Árabe

Encantadas

The Gorge

Los Cotos

El Polvorín

Makinodromo

Desplomilandia

Abdalajís

El Torcal

V. de Cauche

Archidona

Loja

Mijas

Turon

Frontales

Escalera Arabe

Encantadas

The Gorge

Los Cotos

El Polvorin

Makinodromo

Desplomlandia

Abdalajis

El Torcal

V. de Cauche

Archidona

Loja

Gear

Virtually all the routes in this book are single-pitch sport routes protected by bolts. For climbing these you will need a set of around 12 to 18 quickdraws and a single rope. There are a number of multi-pitch climbs that require a rack of nuts and cams but many of these routes do have a smattering of bolts for both protection and belays. Routes which need gear are denoted with the  symbol.

Ropes

A 60m single rope is advised for most routes in this book. You will be able to get up, and more importantly down, many routes on a 50m rope, but it is much safer to use a longer rope. If you intend to climb any multi-pitch routes - sport or trad - then you may wish to take an extra 50m x 9mm rope for the abseil descents.

Other Gear

Beyond these essentials you may find tape useful for bandaging your fingers if the prickly rock starts to take its toll. For multi-pitch routes a small sack with a water bladder, a long-sleeve shirt and a sun hat are good ideas. A good pair of approach shoes are also worth packing as a number of the walk-ins such as that to Makinodromo are long and on scree.

Grades

The routes in El Chorro are graded using the usual sport grade. Over the years El Chorro has had a reputation for slightly softer grades than elsewhere in Spain. Most of those routes should now have been brought back in line with other areas although there may be the odd 'soft touch' out there for you to track down!

Colour Coding

The routes are colour-coded corresponding to a grade band.
Green Spots - Everything at grade 4+ and under. Mostly these should be good for beginners and those wanting an easy life.
Orange Spots - 5 to 6a+ inclusive. General ticking routes for those with more experience.
Red Spots - 6b to 7a inclusive. Routes for the very experienced and keen climber.
Black Spots - 7a+ and above. The hard stuff!

Route Grades

Sport Grade	British Trad Grade (for well protected routes only)	UIAA	USA
1	Mod (Moderate)	I	5.1
2	Diff (Difficult)	II	5.2
2+	VDiff (Very Difficult)	III	5.3
3	HVD (Hard Very Difficult)	III+	5.4
3+	Sev (Severe)	IV	5.5
4	HS (Hard Severe) — VS 4a	IV+	5.6
4+	VS (Very Severe) 4c	V	5.7
5		VI-	5.8
5+	HVS (Hard Very Severe) 5b — E1 5a	VI	5.9
6a	E1 5c	VI	5.10a
6a+	E2 5b	VI+	5.10b
6b	E2 6a — E3 5c	VII-	5.10c
6b+	E3 6a	VII	5.10d
6c	E4 6a	VII+	5.11a
6c+	E4 6b — E5 6a	VIII-	5.11b
7a	E5 6a	VIII	5.11c
7a+	E5 6c	VIII+	5.11d
7b	E6 6b	IX-	5.12a
7b+	E6 6c	IX-	5.12b
7c	E6 6c	IX	5.12c
7c+	E7 6c	IX+	5.12d
8a	E7 7a	X-	5.13a
8a+	E8 6c	X-	5.13b
8b	E8 7a	X	5.13c
8b+	E9 7a	X+	5.13d
8c	E9 7b	XI-	5.14a
8c+	E10 7a	XI	5.14b
9a	E10 7b	XI+	5.14c
9a+		XI+	5.14d
			5.15a

Side tabs: Mijas · Turon · Frontales · Escalera Arabe · Encantadas · The Gorge · Los Cotos · El Polvorin · Makinodromo · Desplomilandia · Abdalajis · El Torcal · V. de Cauche · Archidona · Loja

Mijas

Turon

Frontales

Escalera Arabe

Encantadas

The Gorge

Los Cotos

El Polvorin

Makinodromo

Desplomilandia

Abdalajis

El Torcal

V. de Cauche

Archidona

Loja

Onsighting - *an extract from Sport*CLIMBING+

Whatever your situation you will always have both limited climbing time and limited energy. In our drive to climb lots of great routes, it is tempting to try to onsight everything simply because it is so quick. Below your limit, onsighting is the way to go, covering a lot of ground and gaining valuable experience in movement and boosting your confidence. Closer to your limit a little more thought is required before diving into a hard onsight attempt. Be ambitious, but realistic at the same time. If your hardest recent onsight is 6b, then you'll probably want to push yourself to 6b+, or even 6c if you're feeling confident, and the route favours your strengths. However, it would be an unwise use of time and energy to jump on a 7a, or even a 6b+, that does not suit your style.

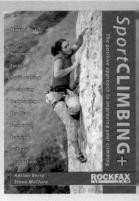

If there's a special route that you really want to climb then be realistic in your style of attack. Assuming you give it your all, and fall at around three-quarter's height, you'll be so tired that it's unlikely you'll have the energy for a redpoint attempt that day. Returning the following day most of the moves will be forgotten and you'll be starting again from scratch. A better strategy would have been to spend the first day working towards a redpoint in the afternoon, with the result that you will save the next day to pursue a more likely onsight prey. An alternative strategy might be to watch someone else on the route and quiz them about the moves – getting 'beta' on how to do it – allowing you the possibility of 'flashing' the route, which might well be within your reach if you get the right 'beta'! Though the onsight is the most coveted style of ascent, the 'flash' is also highly respected and for many the most enjoyable as it gives an onsight 'feel' without missing crucial or unobvious holds.

*Sport*CLIMBING+ is published by Rockfax
and available from **www.rockfax.com**

Mijas

Turón

Frontales

Escalera Árabe

Encantadas

The Gorge

Los Cotos

El Polvorín

Makinodromo

Desplomilandia

Abdalajís

El Torcal

V. de Cauche

Archidona

Loja

Gavin Symonds on *La conexión pelirroja* (8a) - *page 152*
- on El Triangulo at Desplomilandia. Photo: Dave Pickford

Mid crux on *Viejos y puretas* (7a) - *page 157* - on sector Buena Sombra, Desplomilandia. Photo: Mark Glaister

There are a couple of other local guidebooks that are worth a look for those interested in exploring the area in more detail. All of the books are available locally or via a search on the web.

Andalucia, Guia de escalada deportiva (2007)
by David Munilla, Ediciones Desnivel
A huge guidebook of drawn topos covering a vast amount of the climbing in Andalucia. The number of climbs is astonishing and the approach descriptions to the crags reasonably accurate, however no details on the quality or style of the individual climbs is presented. The book has lots of superb colour photos of the harder climbs. In both Spanish and English.

El Chorro, Escalada en Málaga (2007)
by Javier Romero Rubiols
The local guidebook to El Chorro and Desplomilandia. The routes are presented in colour photo and drawn topo form but no details on the quality or style of the individual climbs is given, although a gear list is included for the traditional climbs. In both Spanish and English and available locally.

Mijas

Turon

Frontales

Escalera Arabe

Entantadas

The Gorge

Los Cotos

El Polvorin

Makinodromo

Desplomilandia

Abdalajis

El Torcal

V. de Cauche

Archidona

Loja

Scott Sadler on *Los genelos* (6c) - *page 94* - at the base of El Navegador Pillar, Escalera Arabe. Photo: Mike Hutton

Mijas | Turon | Frontales | Escalera Arabe | Encantadas | The Gorge | Los Cotos | El Polvorin | Makinodromo | Desplomilandia | Abdalajis | El Torcal | V. de Cauche | Archidona | Loja

Alison Martindale climbing the superb tufa pipes of *Hasta luego Luca* (7b) - *page 197* - at Loja. Photo: Mark Glaister

This list contains 50 of the most popular routes in this guidebook. They are not necessarily the best 50, but they are amongst the most coveted. On the Rockfax web site - **www.rockfax.com** - you can vote on the quality of the routes you have climbed. These votes will be used in future as the basis of this list.

	Route	Grade	Photos	Page
☐	Orujo *Archidona*	9a+		186
☐	Cous cous *Makinodromo*	8c		144
☐	Trango *Frontales*	8b+		81
☐	Mar de Ortigas *Desplomilandia*	8a		152
☐	Musas inquientantes *The Gorge*	8a		116
☐	Lourdes *Makinodromo*	8a	opposite	144
☐	Atlas Shrieked *Makinodromo*	7c+		145
☐	Danza agresiva *Archidona*	7c	178	187
☐	Madre Salvaje *Desplomilandia*	7c		152
☐	Honk Down *Frontales*	7c		77
☐	Viejo traidor *Frontales*	7b+		79
☐	The Speed Kings *Makinodromo*	7b+		142
☐	Hasta luego Luca *Loja*	7b	above, 188	197
☐	Akira *Desplomilandia*	7b		153
☐	Diedre candela *Villanueva de Cauche*	7a+	183	183
☐	Hakuna mata *Makinodromo*	7a+		146
☐	Cosas caseras *Desplomilandia*	7a+		157
☐	Sara *Las Encantadas*	7a+		102
☐	Tipo sueca *The Gorge*	7a		116
☐	Poema de Roca P1 *Frontales*	7a		79

Mijas

Turón

Frontales

Escalera Árabe

Encantadas

The Gorge

Los Cotos

El Polvorín

Makinodromo

Desplomilandia

Abdalajís

El Torcal

V. de Cauche

Archidona

Loja

The best known route at El Chorro *Lourdes* (8a) -
page 144 - at Makinodromo. Photo: Mark Glaister

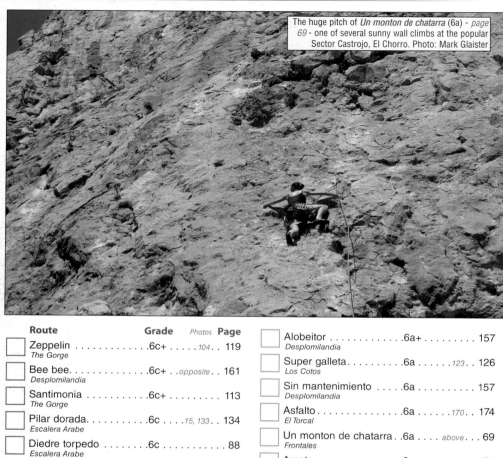

The huge pitch of *Un monton de chatarra* (6a) - *page 69* - one of several sunny wall climbs at the popular Sector Castrojo, El Chorro. Photo: Mark Glaister

Route	Grade	Photos	Page
Zeppelin *The Gorge*	6c+	104	119
Bee bee. *Desplomilandia*	6c+	*opposite*	161
Santimonia *The Gorge*	6c+		113
Pilar dorada. *Escalera Arabe*	6c	15, 133	134
Diedre torpedo *Escalera Arabe*	6c		88
Life is Sweet *Makinodromo*	6c	136	146
Generacion spontanea *El Polvorin*	6c	6	134
Yogur de Coco *Desplomilandia*	6c	148	157
La sonrisa vertical. *Escalera Arabe*	6c		94
Africa. *The Gorge*	6b+	115	114
Buena sombre. *Desplomilandia*	6b+		157
Debora cuerpos *Desplomilandia*	6b		157
Sueno de Venus *El Polvorin*	6a+		134
Fisuras armoniosas. *Valle de Abdalajis*	6a+	162	166
Patranas *Loja*	6a+	191	193
Alobeitor *Desplomilandia*	6a+		157
Super galleta. *Los Cotos*	6a	123	126
Sin mantenimiento *Desplomilandia*	6a		157
Asfalto. *El Torcal*	6a	170	174
Un monton de chatarra. *Frontales*	6a	*above*	69
Amptrax. *Frontales*	6a		71
Putifero *Frontales*	5+		70
Treprorzas *Loja*	5+		192
Floja y pendulona *Túron*	5+	59	57
Cursillos *Los Cotos*	5		126
Julay lama. *Túron*	5	52	57
Number One *Los Cotos*	4+	120	126
Un pobre infeliz. *Valle de Abdalajis*	4+		167
Rogelio *Escalera Arabe*	4+		92
Los timbales *Escalera Arabe*	4		92

Mijas | Túron | Frontales | Escalera Arabe | Encantadas | The Gorge | Los Cotos | El Polvorin | Makinodromo | Desplomilandia | Abdalajis | El Torcal | V de Cauche | Archidona

Mijas

Turon

Frontales

Escalera Arabe

Encantadas

The Gorge

Los Cotos

El Polvorin

Makinodromo

Desplomilandia

Abdalajis

El Torcal

V. de Gauche

Archidona

Loja

Mark Glaister on *Bee bee* (6c+) - *page 161* - at Poza de la Mona at Desplomilandia. Photo: Glaister collection

	Routes	up to 4+	5 to 6a+	6b to 7a	7a+ and up
Mijas	54		26 ✓✓	24 ✓✓	4 ✓
Túron	60		19 ✓✓	26 ✓✓	15 ✓
Frontales	141	11 ✓	35 ✓✓	39 ✓✓	56 ✓✓✓
Escalera Arabe	80	14 ✓✓	26 ✓✓	27 ✓✓	13 ✓✓
Las Encantadas	36	1	8 ✓	10 ✓✓	17 ✓✓✓
The Gorge	94		13 ✓	38 ✓✓	43 ✓✓
Los Cotos	66	2 ✓	30 ✓✓✓	29 ✓✓	5
El Polvorin	16		5 ✓✓	10 ✓✓✓	1
Makinodromo	92		3	22 ✓✓	67 ✓✓✓
Desplomilandia	138		26 ✓✓	45 ✓✓✓	67 ✓✓✓
Valle de Abdalajis	44	14 ✓✓✓	24 ✓✓	6 ✓	
El Torcal	56		12 ✓✓	26 ✓✓	18 ✓✓
Villanueva de Cauche	35		4 ✓	15 ✓✓	16 ✓✓
Archidona	29	2	1	2 ✓	24 ✓✓✓
Loja	106		8 ✓✓	32 ✓✓	66 ✓✓✓

Quality and range of routes in different grade bands: ✓✓✓ - Excellent, ✓✓ - Good, ✓ - Okay, NO TICK - Not worth a visit

Mijas · Turon · Frontales · Escalera Arabe · Encantadas · The Gorge · Los Cotos · El Polvorin · Makinodromo · Desplomilandia · Abdalajis · El Torcal · V. de Cauche · Archidona · Loja

Approach	Sun	Multi-pitch	Dry	Shelter	Windy	Summary	Page	
Roadside	Sun and shade			Sheltered		Situated high up on a hill overlooking the Med, and on the edge of the popular tourist village of Mijas. The climbing is good but the location leaves a bit to be desired. A possible dry spot if the mountains are wet.	44	Mijas
5 to 10 min	Sun and shade	Multi-pitch				A remote area with far reaching views and some incredible limestone slabs that should not be missed. The steeper climbs are not as good as those found elsewhere.	52	Turon
2 to 15 min	Lots of sun	Multi-pitch	Dry in the rain			A huge wall of rock that overlooks the village of El Chorro. One of Europe's great climbing cliffs that offers both single and multi-pitch classics throughout the grades.	62	Frontales
25 to 30 min	Lots of sun	Multi-pitch				One of the nicest places to climb in El Chorro being set away from the main village crags and with extensive views from the crag base. Lots of brilliant pitches for all to enjoy.	82	Escalera Arabe
4 min	Lots of sun					A classy roadside venue that is as good as it appears on first viewing. There have been access problems in the past but these have now eased. Please follow the approach description carefully.	96	Encantadas
12 to 30 min	Sun and shade	Multi-pitch			Windy	The walls and interior of The Gorge are lined with lots of super exposed climbs both traditional and bolted. The access via the 'Camino del Rey' is unique and should not be missed.	104	The Gorge
5 min	Lots of sun			Sheltered		A major venue for those who like their climbing on the friendly side of vertical. Many of the climbs are outstanding but will only be enjoyed by those who possess good technique and footwork. A tranquil and sunny location.	120	Los Cotos
25 min	Afternoon					A great wall of well-featured rock that gives some of the most sustained and varied climbing anywhere. A good place for the fit but not a place to get fit!	130	El Polvorin
30 to 60 min	Lots of sun		Dry in the rain			The toughest and most famous of El Chorro's crags that lives up to its reputation. Some of the newer areas on the escarpment are now starting to gain in popularity.	136	Makinodromo
3 to 4 min	Not much sun		Dry in the rain		Windy	A magical area not far from El Chorro but in a very different setting. Lots of great routes with plenty of mileage available in the mid and upper grades. A good retreat if things are very hot down in El Chorro.	148	Desplomilandia
3 min	Lots of sun					The easy-angled walls on the outskirts of Valle de Abdalajis are only a short drive from El Chorro and are home to plenty of lower and mid-grade sport routes. The views are superb and it is an all-day sun venue.	162	Abdalajis
0 to 10 min	Lots of sun				Windy	Set on top of a 1000m mountain, the weirdly-eroded pinnacles of El Torcal provide lots of climbs in a very unusual environment. This is not a good place to head for in cool weather but is ideal during warm periods.	170	El Torcal
3 min	From mid morning			Sheltered		An attractive wall of vertical limestone that has easy access and a stunning outlook. Most of the climbing is technical and sustained which combined with the crag's aspect makes finding optimum conditions tricky in warm weather.	178	V. de Cauche
5 min	Not much sun		Dry in the rain	Sheltered		An awesome crag with some of Spain's most impressive sport climbs within its confines. The cave faces north and stays dry in the rain.	186	Archidona
0 to 5 min	Not much sun		Dry in the rain		Windy	A fine two-tier crag that has a number of stunning climbs that are usually in condition in warmish weather. Another great crag with a great view.	188	Loja

Mijas

Mijas

Turon

Frontales

Escalera Arabe

Encantadas

The Gorge

Los Cotos

El Polvorin

Makinodromo

Despichelandia

Abdalajis

El Torcal

V. de Cauche

Archidona

Loja

Mijas

Túron

Frontales

Escalera Arabe

Encantadas

The Gorge

Los Cotos

El Polvorin

Makinodromo

Desplomilandia

Abdalajis

El Torcal

V. de Cauche

Archidona

Loja

Arran Deakin on *Condon roto* (6c) - *page 50* -
at the Ravine, Mijas, Photo: Mark Glaister

The small collection of climbs on the cliffs that fringe the tourist mecca of Mijas are minor when compared to the grand crags around El Chorro village to the north, however their proximity to the coast and ease of access, along with a more reliable climate has ensured that the climbs remain popular. Unfortunately, although offering spectacular views of the coast, and being within a few metres of the picture-postcard centre of Mijas, the setting of the climbs is fairly dismal. The Ravine is a dirty and at times smelly spot and the other sectors also have their own problems in the form of litter and dog mess. On the plus side the climbs themselves are on excellent solid rock and offer something to go at for most mid-grade climbers. In a better location the routes would be highly regarded.

There are no access problems at the present time although climbing has been banned here in the past. Please park carefully and keep noise to a minimum.

Approach

From Malaga, follow the A7 towards Marbella and after around 25km, turn off for Mijas (there are two exits so if you miss the first then take the next one which is actually a slightly better road). Both roads wind uphill to a petrol station and roundabout on the edge of Mijas. Go left following a sign for the centre and where the road forks take the right fork. The narrow road becomes cobbled and even narrower but keep on going until the road starts to drop down out of the centre and a one-way sign takes you right. Follow the one-way signs until the crags are visible up and on your left. Drive up to the crag and park carefully either on the road or take the track to the right below the cliff to more parking spots near to the donkey stables.

Conditions

The area gets less rain than most of the other crags in this book and is slightly warmer. The cliffs above the track get the afternoon sun but the Ravine only sees the sun for a few hours in the middle of the day.
There is no chance of climbing here in the rain but the crags do dry quickly.

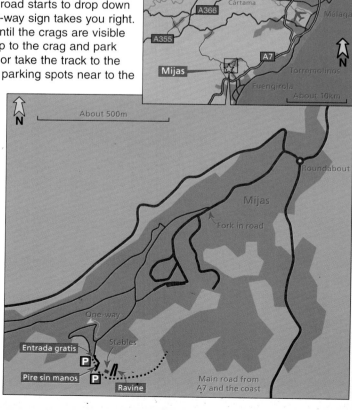

Marti Hallett midway up *Entrada gratis* (7a) - *page 48* - the best pitch at Mijas. Photo: Mark Glaister

Mijas
Turon
Frontales
Escalera Arabe
Encantadas
The Gorge
Los Cotos
El Polvorin
Makinodromo
Desplomilandia
Abdalajis
El Torcal
V. de Cauche
Archidona
Lola

Sector entrada gratis

The best climbing at Mijas is on these two adjoining buttresses of contrasting rock. The left buttress is composed of flowstone and pocketed rock and is severely undercut, whilst the right-hand side is slabbier and compact. The road is very little used but great care should be taken when belaying on the left-hand routes as the rock overhangs the road.

There are no access problems but residential housing is close by so please keep noise to a minimum.

❶ Los Hippy no van tripy

. . . . 7c+

20m. Use a bolt-on hold in the roof to start. Traverse left under the lip, past the arete, then gain the wall above to finish.

❷ Tri-roc, el autentico pirre Americano

. . . . 7b

18m. Use the bolt-on to gain the lip and traverse left until a move can be made onto the wall. Climb the right-hand side of the arete.

❸ Entrada gratis. 7a

16m. Using the bolt-on hold in the roof. Pull straight through the roof and climb the excellent shallow groove above.
Photo on page 47.

❹ El monodedo asesino . . 7b

16m. Pull through the roof as for *Entrada gratis* and then follow the line to its right through bulges.

❺ Si dios existe, es su problema

. . . . 7b

16m. Make difficult moves through the initial overhangs, past an old thread, and continue up the wall directly above.

❻ Sube su puleva. . . . . 6b+

16m. A worthwhile pitch. Move through the bulges and climb up until better holds out right are reached at some pockets. Continue leftwards and up to finish.

❼ Jack el destrepador. . . . . 6a+

17m. Pull through the bulge and head right and up, past another bulge with pockets, and finish direct.

❽ Homosexuales en accion 5+

16m. Pull up through the bulges and move left to jugs that end at an undercut. Follow the difficult wall above to finish.

❾ Virgin ayer, puta hoy. . . . . . 6a+

17m. Climb *Homosexuales en accion* through the bulges and then take the wall on the right to finish.

❿ Alex 6b

17m. The line on the far right of the first wall.

The next routes are just right of the vegetated corner on the compact and less steep buttress.

⓫ Que te den por culo, cara culo

. . . . 6c

17m. A tough cookie. Climb up ledges and a short wall to another ledge. Climb the wall above, on good hidden finger holds, to a hard final section through a bulge.

⓬ Lombrices anales . . 6b+

17m. Climb insecurely up the centre of the slab.

⑬ On parle francais mijeno
. . . . 5+
17m. A delicate and sustained line up the right-hand side of the slab. Start with an awkward pull onto the slab itself.

⑭ Derrape por llevar tenis 6a
20m. A pitch of two halves. Climb up the left side of the leaning arete, then follow the slabby left-hand face. It can be started on the right at the same grade.

To the right is a boulder-sized section of crag with some very short and very steep bolted problems that are not described here.

Sector Pire sin manos

⑮ Mierda de perro . . . 7a
16m. Follow the left edge of the wall on small holds.

⑯ Pues comprate un gusano 6c
16m. A good route that starts up the fingery groove to the right of the arete.

⑰ Quiero follar! 7a
16m. The bulging blunt rib is a touch manufactured.

⑱ Pire sin manos . . . . 6b+
16m. Start easily up the flowstone until a difficult section gains an easing. Above still delicate climbing remains to finish.

⑲ San Miguel . . . . 6c+
16m. Large holds lead to a tricky finish.

Sector Pire sin manos
A good wall that has a number of difficult face climbs spread across it, plus one well-positioned easier line. The wall is situated 60m further down the track a short way up a grassy slope.

⑳ Tufa Groove . . . . (6a+)
16m. The tufa groove.

㉑ Tufa Right . . . . (6b+)
16m. The right-hand line breaking out of the tufa groove.

㉒ Kaga hondo 6c
16m. The bulge-laden flowstone face is taken centrally.

㉓ La pullicia me perseguia 6c
16m. The steep arete is both sustained and technical.

㉔ 1,2,3 Metercanas al poder
. . . . 6c+
17m. The wall right of the arete is highly technical.

㉕ Caligula. . . . . 5+
18m. From the arete, climb up and right to the middle of the face. Continue delicately direct to the top. A fine line.

To the right is another very short buttress next to the track with a number of poor bolted lines that are not described here.

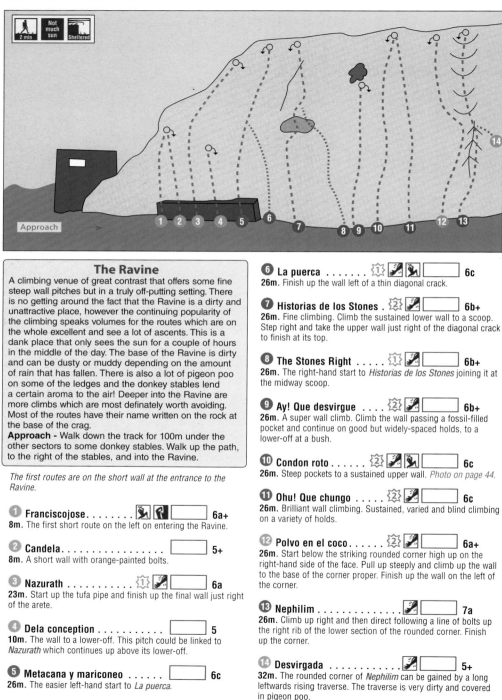

The Ravine

A climbing venue of great contrast that offers some fine steep wall pitches but in a truly off-putting setting. There is no getting around the fact that the Ravine is a dirty and unattractive place, however the continuing popularity of the climbing speaks volumes for the routes which are on the whole excellent and see a lot of ascents. This is a dank place that only sees the sun for a couple of hours in the middle of the day. The base of the Ravine is dirty and can be dusty or muddy depending on the amount of rain that has fallen. There is also a lot of pigeon poo on some of the ledges and the donkey stables lend a certain aroma to the air! Deeper into the Ravine are more climbs which are most definately worth avoiding. Most of the routes have their name written on the rock at the base of the crag.

Approach - Walk down the track for 100m under the other sectors to some donkey stables. Walk up the path, to the right of the stables, and into the Ravine.

The first routes are on the short wall at the entrance to the Ravine.

❶ Franciscojose . . . . 6a+
8m. The first short route on the left on entering the Ravine.

❷ Candela . . . . 5+
8m. A short wall with orange-painted bolts.

❸ Nazurath 6a
23m. Start up the tufa pipe and finish up the final wall just right of the arete.

❹ Dela conception 5
10m. The wall to a lower-off. This pitch could be linked to *Nazurath* which continues up above its lower-off.

❺ Metacana y mariconeo 6c
26m. The easier left-hand start to *La puerca.*

❻ La puerca 6c
26m. Finish up the wall left of a thin diagonal crack.

❼ Historias de los Stones . 6b+
26m. Fine climbing. Climb the sustained lower wall to a scoop. Step right and take the upper wall just right of the diagonal crack to finish at its top.

❽ The Stones Right . . . . . 6b+
26m. The right-hand start to *Historias de los Stones* joining it at the midway scoop.

❾ Ay! Que desvirgue . . . . 6b+
26m. A super wall climb. Climb the wall passing a fossil-filled pocket and continue on good but widely-spaced holds, to a lower-off at a bush.

❿ Condon roto 6c
26m. Steep pockets to a sustained upper wall. *Photo on page 44.*

⓫ Ohu! Que chungo 6c
26m. Brilliant wall climbing. Sustained, varied and blind climbing on a variety of holds.

⓬ Polvo en el coco . . . . . . 6a+
26m. Start below the striking rounded corner high up on the right-hand side of the face. Pull up steeply and climb up the wall to the base of the corner proper. Finish up the wall on the left of the corner.

⓭ Nephilim 7a
26m. Climb up right and then direct following a line of bolts up the right rib of the lower section of the rounded corner. Finish up the corner.

⓮ Desvirgada . . . . 5+
32m. The rounded corner of *Nephilim* can be gained by a long leftwards rising traverse. The traverse is very dirty and covered in pigeon poo.

Mijas

Turon

Frontales

Escalera árabe

Encantadas

The Gorge

Los Cotos

El Polvorin

Makinodromo

Desfiladerolandia

Abdalajís

El Torcal

V. de Cuevas

Archidona

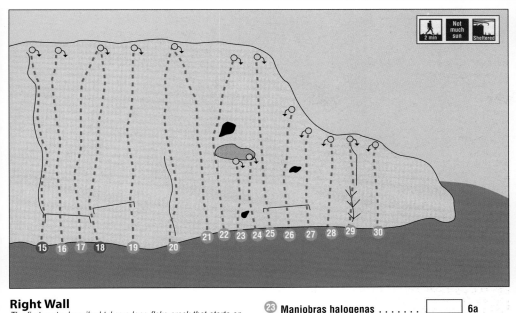

Right Wall
The first route described takes a long flake-crack that starts on the left-hand side of a low ledge.

15 Vuelos Iberia . . . . 🔁 ⚡ [   ] **6b**
26m. The long flake-crack in its entirety.

16 Caca en el culo . . . . . 🔁 ⚡ [   ] **6a**
26m. The wall to the right of the flake-crack has more holds than a first glance suggests and is typical of the climbing on this section of the Ravine.

17 Torpedo nigeriano . . . . 🔁 ⚡ [   ] **6a+**
26m. The blank wall above the low ledge.

18 Funeraria nacional . 🔁 ⚡ 🔦 [   ] **6c**
25m. The wall passing some flowstone ribs.

19 La rebelion de Rasputin . . . 🔁2 [   ] **6a+**
25m. The line of thin seams to the top.

20 Via de Jesus . . . . 🔁2 ⚡ [   ] **5+**
25m. The steepening wall starting up a thin crack, followed by a slight deviation to the right. A good route and easier than it looks.

21 Fuerza, voluntad y huevos . . 🔁 [   ] **6a**
25m. The wall left of the mid-height scoop.

22 Enrique . . . . 🔁 ⚡ [   ] **5+**
24m. Climb to the mid-height scoop and press on past a small cave to the top.

23 Maniobras halogenas . . . . . . [   ] **6a**
9m. A short line past a low hole to a lower-off in the middle of the mid-height scoop.

24 Pablo . . . . [   ] **5**
10m. The wall past the right side of the low hole to a lower-off on the right side of the mid-height scoop.

25 Sueno de Andre . . . . . 🔁 ⚡ [   ] **6a**
21m. Follow the pockets up the wall just right of the scoop.

26 Beat skala bein . . . . 🔦 [   ] **6a**
10m. The wall to the left of a hole.

27 Ana Belen . . . . [   ] **5+**
8m. Thin seams to a chain at a block.

28 No fotis . . . . [   ] **5+**
6m. The short blank wall.

29 La luz del senor . . . . [   ] **5**
6m. The groove and crack.

30 De Carmen . . . . [   ] **5+**
5m. The wall on bore-hole strikes.

Mijas

Túron

Frontales

Escalera Árabe

Encantadas

The Gorge

Los Cotos

El Peñvron

Makinodromo

Desplomilandia

Abdalajís

El Torcal

V. de Cauche

Archidona

Loja

Slabby limestone pitches rarely come better than those on display at Túron.
The route is *Julay lama* (5+) - *page 57*. Photo: Mark Glaister

Túron

Mijas

Túron

Frontales

Escalera Árabe

Encantadas

The Gorge

Los Cotos

El Polverin

Makinodromo

Desplomilandia

Abdalajis

El Torcal

V. de Cauche

Archidona

Loja

The massive slabby limestone sheets of Túron West are some of the region's most distinctive formations and provide many superb climbs in the lower-to-mid grades. The crags are only a short drive away from El Chorro, close to the picturesque Andalucían village of Ardales, and the environment is in complete contrast to The Gorge being more open, rural and tranquil. The West Buttresses are by far and away the most popular areas having the best climbs, although the more intimidating East Buttress is worth a look especially for those looking for morning shade or some harder climbs. Since the last Rockfax guide there has been a lot of rebolting on the West Buttress that has rationalized many of the lines on the slabs. As a consequence of this some of the names painted (or on plaques) at the base of the climbs do not correspond to the current route grades. In some cases the newly rebolted routes are more direct lines and do not follow the older lines that linked discernible features.

Approach

From El Chorro, cross the dam, turn right and drive up the windy road for about 5km to a T-junction. Turn left here and continue about another 5km to Ardales. Drive into the village on the main road, up a hill and into a small open square in the centre. Turn right and immediately pick up a sign for El Burgo. This takes you left into a narrow street and out of the village and into the hills. Follow the road for 6.5km until the crags come into view. Ardales is in the process of having a small ring-road built that will mean that it will not be necessary to go into the centre of the town, just follow signs for 'El Burgo'.

Túron West - Drive past the crags and take the second track on the right (the first track has two entrances close together) follow the track until it drops down to a small bridge over a stream and park on the left. Walk over the bridge towards the farm and then walk right along the side of the first large farm building, passing through makeshift gates, until a track leads to a metal ruin. The crag is easily gained from here via various paths. The access through the farm may change but the farmer is very friendly.

Túron East - Turn left onto a dirt track (this turn off is 1.6 km back towards Ardales from the viewpoint for Túron West). Follow this for 1km to parking on top of the crag. Take a path that drops steeply down the northern flank of the cliff to its base.

Conditions

The West Buttress is slightly lower-lying and receives sun from early morning until late afternoon. The East Buttress is slightly higher and very exposed to the elements, it is also in the shade until mid-afternoon making this a good crag in warm weather. Túron is not the place to be in rain or wind as there is little in the way of shelter, or overhanging rock.

Pippa Froggatt stepping up on *Quasimodo* (6c) - *page 57*
- one of the steeper pitches at Túron. Photo: Chris Sims

Mijas

Túron

Frontales

Escalera Árabe

Encantadas

The Gorge

Los Cotos

El Polvorin

Makinudroma

Desplomilandia

Abdalajis

El Torcal

V. de Cauche

Archidona

Loja

West Buttress

The West Buttress has the most popular routes. The left area is made up of some steep walls in a gully that is worth investigating. The central area of the crag is its showpiece slab of beautiful stone flanked on either side by shorter but harder climbing.

Approach - All routes are accessed from a network of small paths beneath the crag.

❶ Dónde están mis amigos 6c
10m. The steep line of pockets on the arete.

❷ Potage de lentejas . . . . 6c+
10m. The bulging line of pockets on the grey wall.

❸ Kavernicola 6c
28m. A shady line with some steep moves above mid-height.

❹ Gualtrapidos sin fronteras . . 7a+
28m. Good moves combined with an exciting finish up the steep pillar at the top of the gully.

❺ Bolleré . . . . 6b+
24m. An enjoyable steep slab. The line weaves about.

❻ Chupaté ésa Teresa. 6b
24m. A really high quality pitch up the line of cracks in the pillar.

❼ Teardrop 7a
20m. The blank wall past a teardrop-shaped pocket at mid-height and right of a tree.

❽ La grieta de tu nieta . . . 6b
20m. Pockets and cracks passing a tree on the right.

❾ El payaso decotador 7a
20m. A very thin wall and cracks.

❿ La de paraor 6c
20m. Steep tufas to a lower-off below the roof.

⓫ La de Maria 6c
20m. The blunt arete to a lower-off below the roof.

⑫ Apolonio . . . . 7b+
20m. Great climbing on steep pocketed rock, passing a high hole.

⑬ Los malos también lloran 7a+
22m. Varied and airy climbing through the central overlap on immaculate rock. *Photo on page 1.*

⑭ Quasimodo 6c
22m. Coral-like rock and big pockets. *Photo on page 57.*

⑮ Suspiros nostálgicos . . . 6a+
22m. The leaning corner/groove is a bit crunchy.

The next routes are on the huge sweep of slabs to the right.

⑯ Julay lama . . . . 5+
A stunning climb taking on the massive slab. *Photo on page 52.*
1) 27m, 4+. Move up to the high first bolt and continue past a steepening to easier ground and a stance with a lower-off.
2) 25m, 5+. Climb up the wall and take the last section past the final two bolts well to their right.

⑰ Floja y pendulona . . 5+
28m. An absorbing and technical pitch on wonderful rock. *Photo on page 59.*

⑱ Coxy's Climb . . . . . 6a+
28m. A testing pitch up the eroded runnels on either side of the bolt line.

The next three lines are recently bolted and very direct lines that cross older routes. The names and grades are not known but all the pitches look excellent and in the mid-grades. The first bolts are high so take care.

⑲ High Bolt 1 . . . . (6b+)
30m. Thin line left of a hole.

⑳ High Bolt 2 . . . . . . (6b+)
30m. The right-hand side of the hole.

㉑ High Bolt 3 . . . . . . (6b+)
30m. The wall right of a vegetated patch.

㉒ Acosa y derribo 6a
55m. Passing an overhang high up on the second pitch may well be harder than the grade given. 1) 6a, 2) 5+.

㉓ La prima 5
An old two pitch trad climb that is now dirty and seldom climbed. There is a name plaque at the base. 1) 5, 2) 4+.

A little further to the right is an impressive corner.

㉔ Sombra gris 6b
27m. The smooth grey wall left of the arching corner.

㉕ Diedro polvarea 6a
27m. The arching corner gives powerful climbing.

Floja y pendulona

West Buttress - Right

The right-hand side of the West Buttress has more worthwhile pitches although most are not quite as good as those on the left and central sections. There are some easy multi-pitch traditional routes up the broken and line-less headwall above the slabby central area, that are not described here.

Approach - All routes are accessed from a network of small paths beneath the crag.

❶ Anna . . . . ▢ **6a+**
14m. The wall passing a thread.

❷ Sector Olletas . . . . ▢ **5+**
14m. Climb the cracked wall.

❸ Pitiflan exprés . . . . ▢ **6a+**
15m. The staggered cracks just right of *Sector Olletas.*

❹ La raja del siesso . . . . ▢ **7a**
17m. A hard and sharp start gains easier climbing left of a tree.

❺ Manteca colorá . . . . . . ▢ **6b+**
19m. Steep and very enjoyable climbing on large holds.

❻ Como un burro amarao . ▢ **6c**
20m. A bit of lateral thinking is required on this one.

❼ Paco micro y su niva . . . ▢ **6a+**
25m. A rebolted line with its name painted on the rock.

❽ Lo que no puede sar
. . . . ▢ **7a+**
25m. The very bald high-angled slab.

❾ Condón Goretex ▢ **7b+**
26m. Micro holds. The name is on a plaque at the base.

❿ Me cago en la benemérita . . . . ▢ **6c**
20m. A short hard and isolated line.

⓫ Almoraju . . . . ▢ **6a+**
20m. Worth seeking out. Climb the line left of the nose.

⓬ Agustitu . . . . ▢ **6c**
20m. The right-hand side of the nose is a lot tougher.

⓭ Calostro . . . . ▢ **7a**
25m. A very dirty line up the vertical wall.

⓮ Sabor salado . . . . ▢ **6b+**
50m. A two pitch line starting from the higher terrace further up the hillside. The pitches are **6a+, 6b+.**

A climber starting out on the on technical section of the classic *Floja y pendulona* (5+) - *page 57* - on the West Buttress at Túron. Photo: Mark Glaister

Mijas

Túron

Frontales

Escalera Árabe

Encantadas

The Gorge

Los Cotos

El Polvorín

Makinodromo

Desplomilandia

Abdalajis

El Torcal

V. de Cauche

Archidona

Loja

Left

Centre

More routes - mostly in the upper grades

Approach

5 min — Afternoon

Cabrero Blanco

1 2 3 4 5 **6** 7 8 9 10 11 12

El dia de la bestia

East Buttress

This impressive-looking crag is easily spotted from the road that runs beneath it, but unfortunately on closer inspection it is not quite as good as it would first appear. Nevertheless it is well worth a quick visit to pick off the best on offer and the views are fantastic. The left and central sectors are of most interest to the visitor whilst on the right-hand side of the crag are some much harder climbs that see little if any attention and are not described here.

Approach - From the parking spot on top of the cliff, follow a path that drops steeply down the northern (right looking out) flank of the cliff to its base. The sectors are all easily accessed by a good path that runs along the bottom of the crag.

❶ **Cabrero blanco** . . . . **6a+**
17m. A nicely-positioned route that starts just left of the arete.

❷ **Placa la cascabulla.** **6a+**
20m. Move up a short pinnacle and then climb the face to the right of the arete. The first bolt is very high up.

❸ **La condena** **7a**
20m. Pull up the steep lower wall and then follow the smooth scoop above.

❹ **Ascenso al reino de los ciegos**
. . . . **6c**
22m. The eye-catching thin snaking crack is sustained.

Mijas | Túron | Frontales | Escalera Arabe | Encantadas | The Gorge | Los Cotos | El Polvorin | Makinodromo | Desplomilandia | Abdalajis | El Torcal | V de Cavrhe | Archidona | Loja

Mijas
Túron
Frontales
Escalera Árabe
Encantadas
The Gorge
Los Cotos
El Polvorin
Makinodromo
Desplomilandia
Abdalajís
El Torcal
V. de Cauche
Archidona
Loja

5 Banana melosa . . . . . . 🔆🐾 ☐ **6c**
14m. The short left-leaning thin crack to a lower-off next to a small bush.

6 Estrella del sur . . . . 🔆🐾🐾 ☐ **7b**
20m. The good wall of narrow tufas.

7 Si te quieres comer un higo . . . ☐ **5+**
20m. The left-hand side of the pinnacle via a wide crack.

8 Ensancha el alma . . . . . 🔆🐾 ☐ **6b+**
20m. Start in a cave formed by the back of the pinnacle leaning up against the cliff. Climb the impressive thin crackline.

9 Al filo del escualo . . . . . 🔆🐾 ☐ **6a+**
20m. Hop onto and climb the undercut arete of the large detached pinnacle. The start is desperate for the grade.

10 Mamon no comas aleta de tiburón
. . . . 🔆🐾 ☐ **5+**
19m. The right-hand face of the block.

11 El dia de la bestia . . 🔆🐾🐾 ☐ **7c+**
35m. The towering arete is a magnificent line.

12 Newton's Law . . . . ☐ **(8a?)**
35m. The very blank wall right of the arete.

13 Pato palo . . . . ☐ **6a+**
16m. The left-hand side of the low buttress right of the wide corner crack.

14 Vía del topo . . . . ☐ **6a**
17m. A wall leading to a corner.

15 Última del año . . . . 🔆 ☐ **5+**
17m. The corner passing a red overhang.

16 Todo tiene su fin 🔆🐾🐾🐾 ☐ **8a**
30m. A very fine and thin wall pitch.

17 Vía del maki . . . . . 🔆🐾🐾 ☐ **6c+**
16m. A shorter line past some tiny tufas.

18 Mission Impossible . 🔆🐾🐾 ☐ **8a**
35m. The left-hand line up the blank wall right of *Via del maki*.

19 The New Right . . . . ☐ **(8a?)**
35m. The right-hand line up the blank wall right of *Via del maki*.

20 Cuerpo jodio . . . . 🔆 ☐ **7a+**
1) 7a+, 20m. Climb up via some steep tufas.
2) 6b+, 20m. The corner above to the top.

21 Mustang . . . . 🔆🐾 ☐ **7b**
1) 7b, 22m. Take the overhanging corner past a hole.
2) 6b, 15m. Finish up the weakness above.

22 Que cojones el del palo 🔆🐾 ☐ **7c**
30m. Steep bulging wall and tufas.

Running rightwards from the central section of the crag the climbs are less frequented and the cliff gradually loses height. The first couple of lines are actually multi-pitch but are very dirty whilst a little further on the cliff steepens and has a number of lines in the high 7th grade.

Mijas

Turón

Frontales

Escalera Árabe

Encantadas

The Gorge

Los Cotos

El Polvorín

Makinodromo

Desplomilandia

Abdalajís

El Torcal

V. de Cauche

Archidona

Loja

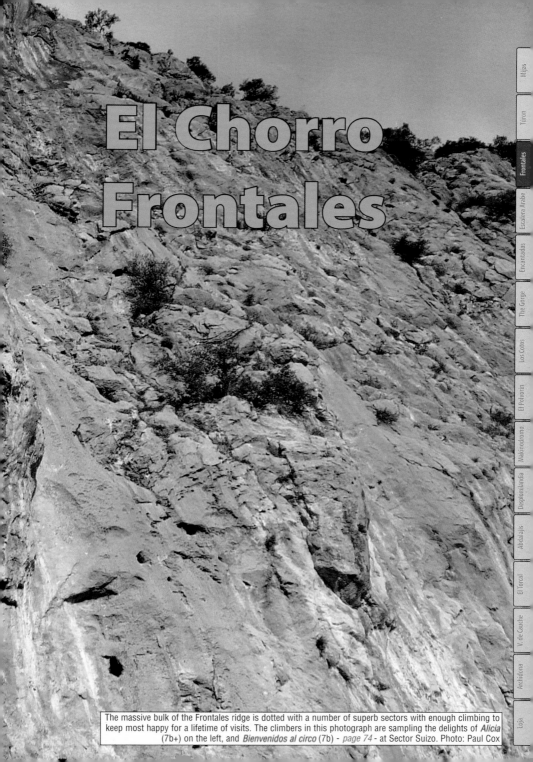

El Chorro
Frontales

Mijas

Turón

Frontales

Escalera Arabe

Encantadas

The Gorge

Los Cotos

El Polvorin

Makinodromo

Desplomilandia

Abdalajís

El Torcal

V. de Cauche

Archidona

Loja

The massive bulk of the Frontales ridge is dotted with a number of superb sectors with enough climbing to keep most happy for a lifetime of visits. The climbers in this photograph are sampling the delights of *Alicia* (7b+) on the left, and *Bienvenidos al circo* (7b) - *page 74* - at Sector Suizo. Photo: Paul Cox

The massive bulk of Frontales looms over the village of El Chorro and offers some of the most important crags in the area. The characteristic cave of Poema de Roca is the eye-catching centrepiece but the walls to either side have a number of fine sectors each with its own varied cluster of routes. The climbing spans all grades and styles varying from slabby to severely overhanging, and from short single pitches to some very extended multi-pitch epics. The easy access and the fact that the Frontales dominates the view from the village, mean that most of the sectors are popular and well-travelled. Since the last edition of the Rockfax guide a lot of climbs have been added to the traditional sectors and a number of new areas have been opened up and development continues at an encouraging rate.

Marti Hallett on pitch 1 of *Poema de Roca* (7a) - *page 79* - Frontales. Photo: Paul Cox

Conditions

Most of the climbing is in the sun from first thing in the morning, however some sectors have trees which give shade low down and many sectors go into the shade in the late afternoon. Rock fall from the vast expanse of rock above the climbs is a small but present danger. On the longer climbs care should be taken to protect against dehydration and sunburn.

Sidebar tabs (left margin): Mijas, Turon, Frontales, Escalera Arabe, Encantadas, The Gorge, Los Cotos, El Polvorin, Makinodromo, Desplomilandia, Abdalajis, El Torcal, V. de Cauche, Archidona, Loja

Panorama labels: Escalera Arabe, Amptrax, Canada, El Olimpo, Austria, Solarium, Poema de Roca, Momia, Suizo, Castrojo, Albercones, P

Approach

There are two basic approaches for the Frontales crags. For the lower sectors from Canada to Momia, the best approach is from the Albercones parking area. This is reached from El Chorro village by following the road which turns off just before the station bar. This leads through the village and on to a dirt track that leads along the side of the campsite to a large parking area just beyond. All the approaches to the various crags are described from the parking area.

For the areas from Poema de Roca to Sector Olimpo, the best approach is to follow the road through the village up the hill towards Valle de Abdalajis. As the road levels out, and just before the large crag of Las Encantadas, park next to a ruined building and water tank. The various approaches to the upper crags are described from this parking.

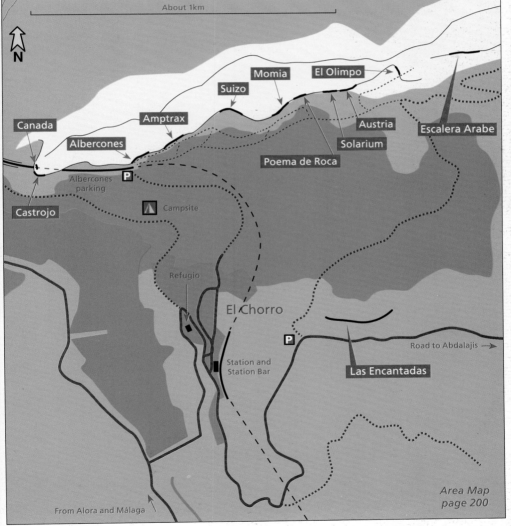

Area Map
page 200

Sector Canada

This section of crag is set high up on the left-hand side of the Frontales ridge but is more awkward to reach than the majority of the older sectors; because of this it tends to be far quieter. The climbs are good but not perhaps quite as good as might be hoped for after the awkward approach - a good place to head for if you want peace and quiet. The crag is a very shady spot until mid afternoon and catches a breeze.

Approach - From the parking area at the fenced-off tunnel entrance, walk along by the side of the fence. Where the tunnel goes into the hillside, traverse left around the rocky shoulder to the start of Sector Castrojo. Climb the route *Access Route for Sector Canada* to a belay as the angle eases and then scramble up the gully into the large bowl beneath the sector itself.

There is loose scree in the gully and a lot of care is needed to not dislodge stones as the gully is directly above some of the climbs on Sector Castrojo.

Mijas · Turon · Frontales · Escalera Arabe · Encantadas · The Gorge · Los Coros · El Polvorin · Makinodromo · Desplomilandia · Abdalajis · El Torcal · V. de Cauche · Archidona · Loja

❶ **El pajaro loco**. . . . . 🔾 ⬚ **7a**
23m. Short line on the far left of the wall.

❷ **Chiguagua** . . . . 🔾 ⬚ **7b**
23m. A steep start up blobs that lead out of the left-hand side of the ground-level cave.

❸ **Vaca loco** . . . . 🔾 ⬚ **7b+**
27m. Start up *Chiguagua* then branch out rightwards.

❹ **Supersonica**. . . . . 🔾 ⬚ **7c**
30m. Take a right-hand diagonal line out of the cave and power up the leaning headwall to a lower-off.

❺ **Riders on the Storm** . . . 🔾 ⬚ **7b+**
30m. Start up *Emmanuelle* and move out on to the left-hand line of bolts. Follow the orange stain to a lower-off shared with *Supersonica*.

❻ **Emmanuelle**. . . . . . 🔾 ⬚ **6c+**
30m. A good sustained wall climb to a steep corner groove.

❼ **Si te vas** . . . . 🔾 ⬚ **7b**
30m. The narrow rib to a hard overhanging headwall.

Mijas

Turón

Frontales

Escalera Árabe

Encantadas

The Gorge

Los Cotos

El Polvorín

Makinodromo

Desplomilandia

Abdalajís

El Torcal

V. de Cauche

Archidona

Loja

Starting out on *Little Brown Baby* (7a+) - *page 69* -
at Sector Castrojo. Photo: Chris Dainton

Classic El Chorro scenery accompanies a climber approaching the high crux of the sustained *Luna* (6a+) - *opposite* - at Sector Castrojo, Frontales. Photo: Mark Glaister

Mijas
Turon
Frontales
Escalera Arabe
Encantadas
The Gorge
Los Cotos
El Polvorin
Makinodromo
Desplomilandia
Abdalajis
El Torcal
V. de Cauche
Archidona
Loja

Sector Castrojo

The first five lines are very easily confused but are all similar in style and are often used by top-ropers hence some of the bolts are for directional purposes only.

1 Estrella . . . . [   ] **4+**
10m. The far left-hand line.

2 Jenny . . . . [   ] **4+**
10m. Climb leftwards on older bolts to the belay of *Estrella*.

3 Randy . . . . [   ] **4+**
9m. A top-rope problem with one bolt low down.

4 Starter. . . . . [   ] **4+**
9m. The line that passes to the left of the tree.

5 Access Route for Sector Canada [   ] **4+**
28m. Climb right of the tree and continue up the gully.

Easy scramble up gully to Sector Canada

Approach

6 Pane pane supermercado 🧗📐/ ☐ **7b+**
28m. The climbing is not as good as it appears.

7 Little Brown Baby ..... ⌂3 📐/ ☐ **7a+**
28m. A sustained and well-travelled favourite. *Photo on page 67.*

8 Simon ha perdido el panadero
. . . . ⌂1 🧗📐 ☐ **6c+**
26m. The corner is hard on its steep upper section.

9 Luna llena . . . . ⌂1 🧗📐/ ☐ **7c**
28m. The leaning blank wall. Sustained to half-height.

10 Instinto . . . . ⌂1 🧗 ☐ **6c**
15m. Steep start to a wall. Polished.

11 Luna . . . . ⌂3 📐/ 🧗 ☐ **6a+**
28m. The first line where the lower bulges fade is an excellent pitch. A high first bolt is tricky to spot. *Photo opposite.*

12 Big Fun . . . . ⌂2 📐/ ☐ **6a+**
30m. An excellent long pitch that has a high first bolt.

13 Un monton de chatarra . Top ⌂50 📐/ ☐ **6a**
35m. Fine sustained moves on lovely rock. *Photo on page 40.*

14 Next Door . . . . ⌂1 🧗📐/ ☐ **6b+**
34m. Start up *Un monton...* to reach a harder upper section.

Photo on page 67.

Sector Castrojo

A pleasantly situated crag with a number of worthwhile single-pitch climbs. Sector Castrojo is one of the most frequented spots in El Chorro being both close to the village and getting the sun from early in the morning.
Approach - From the parking area at the fenced-off tunnel entrance, walk along by the side of the fence. Where the tunnel goes into the hillside, traverse left around the rocky shoulder to the start of the sector.

15 Slipped in . . . . ⌂1 ☐ **5**
11m. The short blunt arete.

16 But One . . . . ⌂1 ☐ **5**
11m. Climb to a lower-off below an overhang.

17 Punto de salida . . . . ⌂1 ☐ **4**
11m. The good short wall is the best of the easier lines.

18 La corona . . . . ⌂1 ☐ **4+**
11m. Climb over the bulge and wall left of the corner of *Vas pisando huevos.*

19 Vas pisando huevos . . . ⌂1 📐/ ☐ **5**
19m. The corner on the right-hand side of the crag.

20 Baron rojo . . . . ⌂1 🧗 ☐ **6b+**
17m. The arete right of the corner of *Vas pisando huevos.*

Sidebar tabs (right margin): Mijas · Turon · Frontales · Escalera Arabe · Encantadas · The Gorge · Los Cotos · El Polvorin · Makinodromo · Desplomilandia · Abdalajis · El Torcal · V. de Gauche · Archidona · Loja

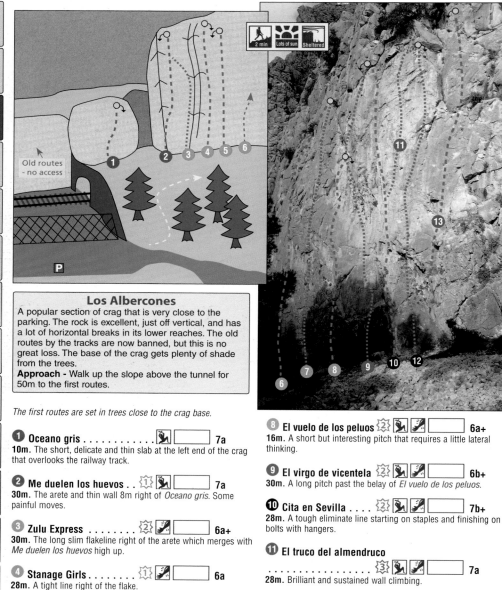

Mijas

Túron

Frontales

Escalera Árabe

Encantadas

The Gorge

Los Cotos

El Polvorín

Makinodromo

Desplomilandia

Abdalajís

El Torcal

V. de Cauche

Archidona

Loja

Old routes - no access

Los Albercones

A popular section of crag that is very close to the parking. The rock is excellent, just off vertical, and has a lot of horizontal breaks in its lower reaches. The old routes by the tracks are now banned, but this is no great loss. The base of the crag gets plenty of shade from the trees.

Approach - Walk up the slope above the tunnel for 50m to the first routes.

The first routes are set in trees close to the crag base.

1 Oceano gris **7a**
10m. The short, delicate and thin slab at the left end of the crag that overlooks the railway track.

2 Me duelen los huevos . . **7a**
30m. The arete and thin wall 8m right of *Oceano gris*. Some painful moves.

3 Zulu Express . . . . **6a+**
30m. The long slim flakeline right of the arete which merges with *Me duelen los huevos* high up.

4 Stanage Girls **6a**
28m. A tight line right of the flake.

5 La chica pelirroja . . . . . **6a+**
28m. The excellent cracked and pocketed wall.

6 Gabi **6a**
30m. A fabulous wall climb passing a left-trending flake midway.

7 Putifero . . . . **5+**
30m. A really excellent long pitch with a tricky start. The route name is written on the rock at the start. High in the grade.

8 El vuelo de los peluos **6a+**
16m. A short but interesting pitch that requires a little lateral thinking.

9 El virgo de vicentela **6b+**
30m. A long pitch past the belay of *El vuelo de los peluos*.

10 Cita en Sevilla . . . . **7b+**
28m. A tough eliminate line starting on staples and finishing on bolts with hangers.

11 El truco del almendruco
. . . . **7a**
28m. Brilliant and sustained wall climbing.

12 Sufre mamon . . . . . **7a+**
28m. The thin wall just left of the arete high up on the crag.

13 Malditos roedores . . . . . **6c+**
30m. The right-trending line to a recessed wall.

Walk and scramble off

Line of
4 x 35m abseil

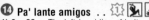

Amptrax

This huge wall dominates the view from the village of El Chorro. The pale line of the popular *Amptrax* can be picked out as the rock has been scoured by the passage of many ascents. The wall has very little shade and is exposed to the elements.

Approach - From the Albercones parking, walk right up a path, over the tunnel, and up the hillside to the Albercones sector. Continue for a further 120m and head up left to an area of ledges from where the routes begin.

Descent - From the top of pitch 5 abseil back down the route, or down an abseil line from the stance at the end of pitch 7.

Walking Descent - From top of the route, scramble up through low bushes (beware loose boulders) to a notch in the skyline. From the notch go right across and slightly down past a cairn to another cairn below another larger notch in the ridge. From here follow cairns down into the gully which leads easily into the valley. Pick up a path to the right of the valley and follow this all the way down to the huge bridge and the railway line. Walk around the outside of the tunnel back to the Albercones Area.

⑭ Pa' lante amigos .. **6c**
1) **6a, 20m.** The left-hand line of bolts.
2) **6c, 30m.** Abseil off or lower back to the first stance.

⑮ Son quatros . . . . **6b+**
1) **4, 15m.** Easy pitch to a stance.
2) **6b+, 35m.** Climb to the lower-off of *Pa' lante amigos*.

⑯ Amptrax. **6a**
This is the most popular multi-pitch climb on Frontales which gives good steep climbing and is fully bolted from pitches 2 to 5. Some gear will be required for the first pitch (which is very easy) and the last three pitches, if intending to go to the top, although many abseil off from the top of pitch 5. Reach the start by scrambling up to the grassy bay above the path beneath a ramp.
1) **3, 35m.** Follow the ramp until you need to put a rope on at a two bolt belay.
2) **5+, 30m.** Move up to two more bolts and a yellow peg. Climb left of a smooth wall and then to the base of a small ramp. Move up right to a bolted stance.
3) **5+, 15m.** Another steep pitch on good holds to a bolted stance on the left.
4) **6a, 16m.** Climb the steep white wall on good but hidden holds to a bolted stance.
5) **6a, 20m.** Climb the wall with difficulty mainly to the left of the bolts. Continue to a bolted stance below the steep headwall. Abseil from here for the sport tick.
6) **5, 25m.** Traverse right past pegs and bolts before moving up to a bolted stance.
7) **4+, 20m.** Climb up then right past an orange bay to a bolted stance just beyond. Abseil from here 4x35m.
8) **4+, 40m.** Move up left and on up to a tree before climbing to the top via walls and ribs that gradually ease.

14   15   16

Approach

Mijas
Turon
Frontales
Escalera Arabe
Encantadas
The Gorge
Los Cotos
El Polvorin
Makinodromo
Desplomilandia
Abdalajis
El Torcal
V. de Cauche
Archidona
Loja

Mijas

Túron

Frontales

Escalera Árabe

Encantadas

The Gorge

Los Cotos

El Polvorín

Makinodromo

Desplomilandia

Abdalajis

El Torcal

V. de Cuiche

Archidona

Sector Suizo

Sector Momia
and

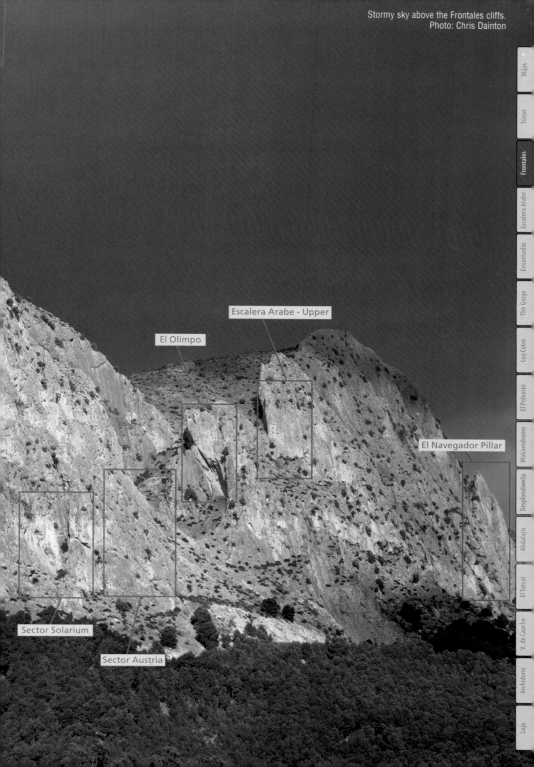

Stormy sky above the Frontales cliffs.
Photo: Chris Dainton

Escalera Arabe - Upper

El Olimpo

El Navegador Pillar

Sector Solarium

Sector Austria

Mijas

Turon

Frontales

Escalera Arabe

Encantadas

The Gorge

Los Cotos

El Polvorin

Makinodromo

Desplomilandia

Abdalajis

El Torcal

V. de Gaucho

Archidona

Loja

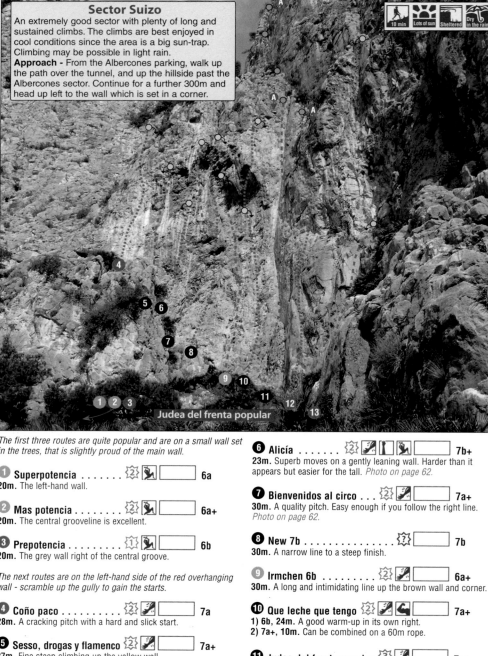

Sector Suizo

An extremely good sector with plenty of long and sustained climbs. The climbs are best enjoyed in cool conditions since the area is a big sun-trap. Climbing may be possible in light rain.

Approach - From the Albercones parking, walk up the path over the tunnel, and up the hillside past the Albercones sector. Continue for a further 300m and head up left to the wall which is set in a corner.

The first three routes are quite popular and are on a small wall set in the trees, that is slightly proud of the main wall.

1 Superpotencia **6a**
20m. The left-hand wall.

2 Mas potencia . . . . **6a+**
20m. The central grooveline is excellent.

3 Prepotencia **6b**
20m. The grey wall right of the central groove.

The next routes are on the left-hand side of the red overhanging wall - scramble up the gully to gain the starts.

4 Coño paco **7a**
28m. A cracking pitch with a hard and slick start.

5 Sesso, drogas y flamenco **7a+**
27m. Fine steep climbing up the yellow wall.

6 Alicía . . . . **7b+**
23m. Superb moves on a gently leaning wall. Harder than it appears but easier for the tall. *Photo on page 62.*

7 Bienvenidos al circo . . . **7a+**
30m. A quality pitch. Easy enough if you follow the right line. *Photo on page 62.*

8 New 7b **7b**
30m. A narrow line to a steep finish.

9 Irmchen 6b . . . . **6a+**
30m. A long and intimidating line up the brown wall and corner.

10 Que leche que tengo **7a+**
1) 6b, 24m. A good warm-up in its own right.
2) 7a+, 10m. Can be combined on a 60m rope.

11 Judea del frenta popular **7a+**
40m. The steep groove right of the red wall is a tremendous line. Double ropes are useful for getting down, otherwise an intermediate lower-off from a single bolt will have to be made.

Tinto de Verano

Lowering-off - Some of these pitches are longer than 30m in length. Take care when lowering off.

Approach

Sector Bridwell

Mijas

Turon

Frontales

Escalera Arabe

Encantadas

The Gorge

Los Cotos

El Polvorin

Makinodromo

Desplomilandia

Abdalajis

El Torcal

V. de Cauche

Archidona

Loja

⑫ Frente popular de Judea

. . . .  **6c**
1) 6b, 40m. The wall to the right of the groove gives a superb pitch. Abseil off or continue up....
2) 6c, 3) 6a, 4) 6a. Three more good pitches above.
Descent - Abseil back down on two 50m ropes.

⑬ Libertad para Maria . . . **6c+**
1) 5, 20m. Climb up the shallow corner to a stance.
2) 6c+, 30m. Climb up holes to a difficult hanging corner.

⑭ Yailhouse rock **6b**
30m. The line just to the right of broken ground.

⑮ Tinto de verano . . . . . . **6a+**
38m. A massive pitch of escalating difficulties.

⑯ No esta acabda . . . **6b+**
40m. Another huge pitch that also has a mid-height lower-off.

⑰ Soñador de grado **4**
18m. This pitch is used to access the following three climbs. Only one bolt to the belay.

⑱ La niña de mis oios . . . **6c+**
30m. The left-hand line up the light-coloured tufas.

⑲ La urriki . . . . **7a+**
30m. The central line up the orange pocketed wall.

⑳ Ajonjoli **8a**
30m. The steep right-hand side of the orange wall.

㉑ Quatro elephants **5**
30m. A nicely situated climb up the right rib of the overhanging orange wall. Reach the start via a traverse along ledges.

Below the approach traverse of *Quatro elephants* is a tiny insignificant set of 7 routes - **Sector Bridwell**. From the left the grades are - **5, 6c+, 5+, 6c+, 6a, 6b+, 5+**. Some bolts are missing.

A
A
A
A
15
5
24
20
18
19
21
22
23
25
14
17
16
8
10
9
11
7
12
13
15
6
5
4
3
2 (10m)
1 (80m)
12 min
Lots of sun
Multi-pitch
Escalera Arabe
Amptrax
Canada
El Olimpo
Austria
Solarium
Suizo
Momia
Poema de Roca
P
Albercones
Castrojo

Sector Momia

The Momia Area is a popular section of the Frontales with a great line-up of long single-pitch climbs. The older multi-pitch lines see little traffic and have dubious bolts. The climbs do go into the shade in the late afternoon. There is little opportunity for climbing in the rain.
Approach - From the Albercones parking, walk right up the path, over the tunnel, and up the hillside under the Albercones sector. Continue for a further 400m and head up left to the climbs. The climbs are also easily reached in a couple of minutes from the Poema Roca cave.

The first two routes are just off the left edge of the topo. Orphan is on the open face between Sector Suizo and the Momia Area.

1 Orphan . . . . 6a+
An isolated face route. Fine climbing. **1)** 6a+, **2)** 6a, **3)** 6a.

2 Gold Bolts . . . . (6a)
A line of gold-coloured bolts. The grade is a guess.

3 Makita Power 6c
30m. An interesting and puzzling route starting up a crack. Don't step right too early.

4 Welcome to El Chorro . . . 5+
28m. Climb the wall to a lower-off.

5 Café burbuscon . . . 7a
A long climb with good first and third pitches plus a wild fourth. The pitch grades are **1)** 5+, **2)** 6c, **3)** 7a, **4)** 6c+.

6 Las carruchas del anakrin 5+
28m. A grey rib to a lower-off.

7 Gaia . . . . 7a+
An old line but a good first pitch. Above there are some rounded holds all topped off with a strenuous overlap. The pitch grades are **1)** 6c, **2)** 7a+, **3)** 6b+. Abseil off.

8 El Orejazo 7a
35m. A long line with steady climbing and prickly rock. Start up the slab.

9 Hamunaptra 7c
40m. A massive steepening line that starts up the right-hand side of a slab.

10 Honk Down 7c
38m. An impressive route. Start up rungs and the deep cleft.

11 Anack Sunamun 7b
32m. Start up the steep tufa on the right wall of cleft. Great varied climbing with no really hard moves.

12 Habana Club 7a
30m. The wide cracks and roof give good climbing but the direct line is an eliminate and much harder than 7a.

13 Insominio de equipmiento 6c+
. . . .
30m. A brilliant and intricate pitch to the lower-off at the top of the first pitch of *Seco y Pedro*. A hard crux move.

14 Fluidos vital 7b
35m. Climb rightwards out of *Insominio de equipmiento* and cross *Seco y Pedro* before finishing directly up a long blank section of wall.

15 Seco y Pedro . . . . . 7a+
A good first pitch (2 stars in its own right) and a quality top pitch.
1) 6b, **30m.** Climb the corner and crack to a lower-off under an overhang. Worth doing for a red spot tick.
2) 6c+, **25m.** Climb up steeply to gain the left-leaning line which leads to a stance.
3) 7a+, **30m.** A long and sustained pitch. Abseil off.

The next route is just left of an arched recess.

16 Out of Vogue . . . . 7a+
A defunct climb with old bolts starting right of a huge cactus. The pitch grades are **1)** 6a, **2)** 6c+, **3)** 7a+.

The large cave-like depression that has some steep lines.

17 Antidoto 8a
24m. Hard climbing up the left side of the cave.

18 El padre Orillos . . . . . . 8a+
24m. The blank cave wall to the same lower-off as *Antidoto*.

19 Black Cave 7b
25m. Steep climbing across the right-to-left line. Often dirty. Possibly only **7a+** when clean.

20 Hora kane . . . . 7b+
23m. The right-hand line midway across the roof of *Black Cave*, past a hanging blob.

The next routes are tricky to identify. There is a report of a new 6 pitch 7c+ that takes a line to the right of El fin de una vida.

21 El fin de una vida 7c
A massive route to the top of the wall. The pitch grades are
1) 7b, **2)** 7a+, **3)** 7b+, **4)** 7c, **5)** 4, **6)** 3, **7)** 6b+, **8)** 6c, **9)** 4.

22 Costris Climbers 7c
26m. Hard climbing up the wall right of the cave.

23 Verdes venenas . . . . . . 7a+
1) 6b, **25m.** An access pitch up the wall right of cave.
2) 7a+, **25m.** The left-hand line from the belay.

24 Hierbes letales . . . . 7a+
25m. An alternative right-hand finish to *Verdes venenas*.

25 Checkout . . . . 6b+
26m. Off-vertical climbing on the grey wall.

Mijas
Turon
Frontales
Escalera Arabe
Encantadas
The Gorge
Los Cotos
El Polvorin
Makinodromo
Desplomilandia
Abdalajis
El Torcal
V. de Cauche
Archidona
Loja

Left sidebar tabs: Mijas, Turon, **Frontales**, Escalera Arabe, Encantadas, The Gorge, Los Cotos, El Polvorin, Makinodromo, Desplomilandia, Abdalajis, El Torcal, V. de Cauche, Archidona, Loja

Line of abseil descent

A

Close-up opposite

El fin de una vida

Poema de Roca

Poema de Roca is the tallest section of the Frontales wall and has a large oval cave at its base - the Poema Cave, one of El Chorro's most famous sections of crag. The climbs are mostly hard and steep, however their quality and popularity, combined with the fact that they rarely get wet, means that they are pretty slick when it is warm. For the majority of climbers the lower wall of the cave is the limit of ambition whilst the extensions that lead out to the cave lip rarely see attempts. Even less frequented are the exceptional long multi-pitch climbs that take on the huge headwall above the cave. The crag goes into the shade in the late afternoon and climbing is possible in the cave in the rain.

Approach - There are two main approaches to the cliff that take about the same length of time, the first being shorter but steeper and the second longer but flatter. **1)** From the Albercones parking, walk right up the path, over the tunnel, and up the hillside to the Albercones sector. Continue for a further 500m and head up left to the Poema Cave. This approach has the advantage of passing lots of the other Frontales sectors.

2) From the station in El Chorro, drive up the road towards Valle de Abdalajis and park at a building next to a water tank, just before Las Encantadas. Take the upper of two dirt tracks on the left and walk along this for 10 minutes until the track meets the hillside at a large quarry. Pick up a path on the left that traverses the steep hillside to the Poema Cave.

Descent - The long routes require multiple abseils on twin 50m ropes to descend.

❶ Kervala **8b**
35m. The smooth streaked wall left of the cave.

❷ Maquina cualquiera . . . **7b+**
The easiest of the big lines. Start at the left edge of the cave.
1) 7a+, 2) 6c+, 3) 7a+, 4) 7b+, 5) 7a+, 6) 6b+. Abseil off.

❸ El complot . . . . **8a+**
27m. Super-steep climbing around the left edge of the cave.

❹ La villa strangiato . . **7b**
15m. Slots and pockets up the left wall of the cave.

❺ Eye of the Storm . . . **7c**
19m. Start up a wide crack at the back of the cave. Very disorientating climbing.

❻ Thunder Struck . . . . **7c+**
19m. Butch climbing to the *Eye of the Storm* lower-off in the middle of the roof.

❼ Swimming Through a Shark Attack
. . . . **8a+**
19m. Steep blobs to the *Eye of the Storm* finish. Brilliant.

❽ Shark Extension . . . **8b**
26m. Connect *Shark Attack* to the first belay of *Maquina*.....

To the right is a long-standing project.

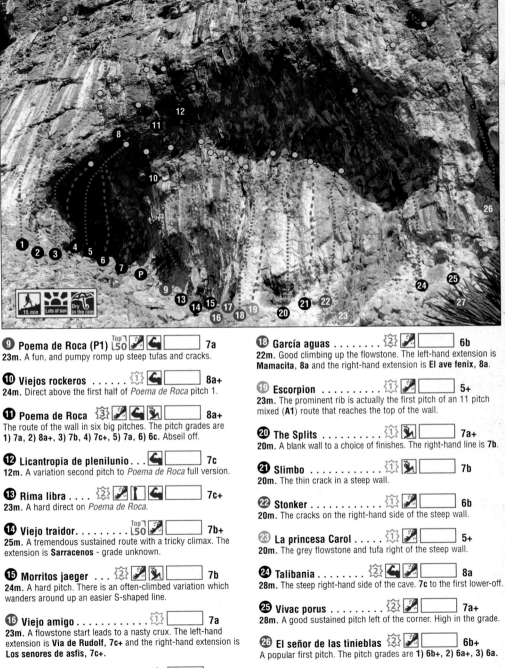

9 Poema de Roca (P1) ⌈Top⌉⌊50⌋ 🔲 **7a**
23m. A fun, and pumpy romp up steep tufas and cracks.

10 Viejos rockeros . . . . . . 🔲 **8a+**
24m. Direct above the first half of *Poema de Roca* pitch 1.

11 Poema de Roca 🔲 **8a+**
The route of the wall in six big pitches. The pitch grades are
1) 7a, 2) 8a+, 3) 7b, 4) 7c+, 5) 7a, 6) 6c. Abseil off.

12 Licantropia de plenilunio . . . 🔲 **7c**
12m. A variation second pitch to *Poema de Roca* full version.

13 Rima libra . . . . 🔲 **7c+**
23m. A hard direct on *Poema de Roca*.

14 Viejo traidor . . . . ⌈Top⌉⌊50⌋ 🔲 **7b+**
25m. A tremendous sustained route with a tricky climax. The
extension is **Sarracenos** - grade unknown.

15 Morritos jaeger . . . 🔲 **7b**
24m. A hard pitch. There is an often-climbed variation which
wanders around up an easier S-shaped line.

16 Viejo amigo . . . . 🔲 **7a**
23m. A flowstone start leads to a nasty crux. The left-hand
extension is **Via de Rudolf**, **7c+** and the right-hand extension is
Los senores de asfis, **7c+**.

17 Newie . . . . 🔲 **6b+**
22m. Left of the flowstone edge of *Garcia aguas*.

18 García aguas . . . . 🔲 **6b**
22m. Good climbing up the flowstone. The left-hand extension is
Mamacita, 8a and the right-hand extension is **El ave fenix, 8a**.

19 Escorpion . . . . 🔲 **5+**
23m. The prominent rib is actually the first pitch of an 11 pitch
mixed (**A1**) route that reaches the top of the wall.

20 The Splits . . . . 🔲 **7a+**
20m. A blank wall to a choice of finishes. The right-hand line is **7b**.

21 Slimbo . . . . 🔲 **7b**
20m. The thin crack in a steep wall.

22 Stonker . . . . 🔲 **6b**
20m. The cracks on the right-hand side of the steep wall.

23 La princesa Carol . . . . . 🔲 **5+**
20m. The grey flowstone and tufa right of the steep wall.

24 Talibania . . . . 🔲 **8a**
28m. The steep right-hand side of the cave. **7c** to the first lower-off.

25 Vivac porus . . . . 🔲 **7a+**
28m. A good sustained pitch left of the corner. High in the grade.

26 El señor de las tinieblas 🔲 **6b+**
A popular first pitch. The pitch grades are **1) 6b+, 2) 6a+, 3) 6a.**

27 Fahrenheit . . . . 🔲 **6c**
10m. The short arete right of the corner.

Mijas
Turon
Frontales
Escalera Arabe
Encantadas
The Gorge
Los Cotos
El Polvorin
Makinodromo
Desplomilandia
Abdalajis
El Torcal
V. de Cauche
Archidona
Loja

There are reports of 3 routes on the far left of this sector, two of which are single 48m pitches, however the rock is poor.

1 Las amigas de Lulu **5**
26m. An easy-angled wall to a lower-off under an overhang.

2 El osito polar **5**
26m. Similar to *Las amigas de Lulu* to same lower-off.

3 Solarium **7b**
28m. Intimidating climbing with a hard clip.

4 Lobo López . . .   **7b**
28m. The right-hand side of the holes. Low in the grade.

5 Clint Eastwood . . . .   **6b+**
A good three pitch line up the arete and wall.
1) 4, 16m. The easy-angled arete to belay.
2) 6b+, 14m. The steeper continuation.
3) 6b, 12m. The wall on the left. Abseil off.

6 Deprisa y con bulla **6c**
16m. Steep, short and thuggy.

7 Agip **6a**
19m. A good little wall of 'Verdon-esque' rock.

8 Billy the Kid . . . . . .   **6a+**
35m. Start up *Agip*, gain and climb the corner above.

9 Nanuz . . . .   **6a+**
20m. Good wall climbing, just left of the corner.

Sector Austria

10 Edelweiss **4**
28m. The easy-angled rib left of the gully.

11 Tall People **6b**
30m. The first line of bolts right of the back of the gully.

12 Small People **6b**
30m. The second line of bolts right of the back of the gully.

13 Wienes Schnitzel . .   **6c**
1) 6b+, 28m. Climb the steep wall just to the right of the huge leaning corner.
2) 6c, 25m. Take the line of bolts above to finish.

14 Full Moon . . . .   **6a+**
1) 6a+, 26m. A steep wall to a stance at break. It can be climbed into *Sumsi* at 5+ to give a shorter and easier pitch.
2) 6a+, 25m. Continue up the grey wall above.

15 Sumsi **4**
20m. The wall to a belay at the steepening.

The Solarium and Sector Austria

These two popular sectors have a good selection of climbs and fine views. The multi-pitch climbs especially are excellent but watch out for loose rock when pulling down abseil ropes. Both sectors dry quickly and gets lots of sun but offers little shade.

Approach - From El Chorro, drive towards Valle de Abdalajis and park at a building by a water tank, just before Las Encantadas. Take the upper of two tracks on the left and walk for 10 minutes until the track meets the hillside at a quarry. Take a path on the left and traverse the hillside towards the Poema Cave. This path takes you under Sector Austria and on to The Solarium.

15 min   Lots of sun

The Solarium

Sector Austria

16 Don Lucas . . . . 🔝 📷 [ ] **6b**
22m. Climb up steeply to a belay under an overhang.

17 Bub oder madl . . . . 🔝 🧗 📷 [ ] **6b+**
20m. Pull through the overhang and head right and up to finish.

18 Mugl . . . . 🔝 📷 [ ] **5+**
21m. Climb up right and then back left to a belay.

19 Finkastinker . . . . 🔝 [ ] **4**
20m. The low-angled wide rib is pleasant.

20 Nitti . . . . 🔝 📷 [ ] **5+**
1) **5+, 20m.** Climb the to a belay ledge in an alcove.
2) **5+, 20m.** Pull up into the corner and follow it to a ledge.

21 Valentines Day . . . . 🔝 📷 [ ] **6a**
A great expedition with good climbing throughout.
1) **4, 40m.** Follow the rounded buttress, corner and wall past a chain to a good ledge and belay.
2) **5+, 40m.** Move up left and climb to a cactus and then follow the crack above to another good ledge and belay.
3) **6a, 25m.** Climb steepening rock on good holds to a belay.
4) **5+, 25m.** Climb on past the final bulges to the top.
Descent - Abseil back down the line.

22 A pique de un repique . . . . . 🧗 [ ] **6c**
17m. The steep line around 60m to the right of the main crag.

El Olimpo

A steep buttress with some great hard routes. It is in the shade until the late afternoon.
Approach - Head up rightwards from the path leading to Sector Austria.

23 La banda del sur . . . . [ ] **8b**
40m. The first line on the right of the steep wall.

24 Endless Power . . . . 🔝 📷 🧗 [ ] **8c+**
40m. The current hardest of the bunch which may only have been done by starting up *Trango*.

25 Trango . . . . 🔝📷 [ ] **8b+**
40m. A magnificent climb. **8a+** to first lower-off.

26 Kukeman tupery . . . . 🔝 [ ] **7c**
35m. The line right of a project can be split.

El Olimpo

Sector Austria

Mijas Turón Frontales Escalera Arabe Encantadas The Gorge Los Cotos El Polvorin Makinodromo Desplomilandia Abdalajis El Torcal V. de Cauche Archidona Loja

El Chorro
Escalera
Arabe

Mijas

Turon

Frontales

Escalera Arabe

Encantadas

The Gorge

Los Cotos

El Polvorin

Makinodromo

Desplomilandia

Abdalajis

El Torcal

V. de Cauche

Archidona

Lola

Expansive views and sustained wall climbing are the norm at Escalera Arabe. *Escalopendra guajan* (6c) - *page 87* - on the upper section of Escalera Arabe. Photo: Chris Dainton

Set high up above the treeline and commanding a beautiful view, the Escalera Arabe is one of El Chorro's most peaceful locations. The quality of the climbing matches the view with the majority of the routes being single-pitch wall climbs on brilliant rock. The best climbs are in the lower-to-mid grade range and there are plenty of them, although there are a number of good harder pitches dotted across the various sectors. In the past it was possible to drive up the track to the base of the cliff, however the track has now been closed by the National Park and as a result the approach is considerably longer on foot although it is a lovely walk and not at all strenuous. There is occasional stone fall from the large areas of broken crags above the climbs and a helmet is advised. The area is named after the Mozarabic stairway built pre-1500, sections of which are still in amazing condition.

Approach

From the station in El Chorro drive up the road towards Valle de Abdalajis and, just before the crag of Las Encantadas, park at a building next to a water tank. Take the upper of two dirt tracks on the left and walk along this for around 10 minutes until the track meets the hillside at a large quarry. Continue up the track that follows the base of the slope below the cliffs for a further 10 minutes until just past the point where a power line crosses over the track and look for paths that head up the slope to the base of the crag itself. For El Navegador Pillar continue up the road to a small hairpin bend and walk up a steep but short path on the left to the cliff. For those without a car it is nicer to walk from the station in the direction of the Albercones parking and just after leaving the built-up area, walk up a track on the right that eventually meets up with the approach track to the quarry.

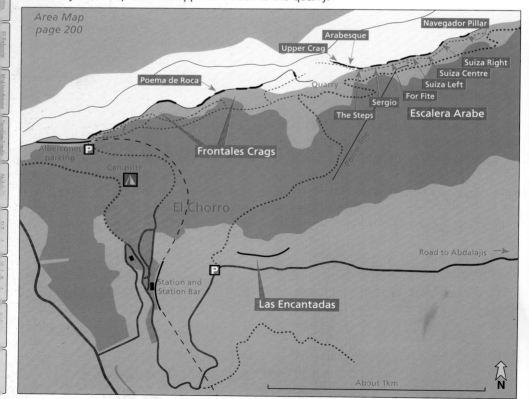

Conditions

All of the climbing at Escalera Arabe is very exposed to the sun and the rain. There is a little bit of shade to be found at various spots along the base of the cliff but the climbs described are in the sun for most of the day. There is no water source at the crag. This is not a good place to head for if the weather is windy or wet although the crags do dry extremely quickly after rainfall and there is little seepage.

Mijas

Turon

Frontales

Escalera Arabe

Encantadas

The Gorge

Los Cotos

El Polvorin

Makinodromo

Desplomilandia

Abdalajis

El Torcal

V. de Cauche

Archidona

Loja

A climber working out the sequence on *Sheik tu dinero* (6c+) - *page 89* - just one of many fantastic mid-grade routes at Escalera Arabe. Photo: Mike Hutton

Upper Crag

A vertical wall and pillar of great rock in a magnificent setting and with some of the finest views in El Chorro. The climbs are either two pitches or very long single pitches and very sustained. There are a number of hard routes that are not described here located on a large and shady face around the back of the Upper Crag that is accessed by walking along the base of the crag to where the cliff fades and then doubling back up to the face.

Approach - The base of the crag is at the top of the steps and has a large pinnacle just in front of the main section of the wall, walk up the steps to reach it.

Lowering-off - Some of these pitches are longer than 30m in length. Take care when lowering off and use the mid-route lower-offs if you are unsure about reaching the ground.

The first two short climbs are 80m to the left of the Upper Crag.

① **Magigi** . . . . ☐ **5+**
10m. The left-hand line.

② **El Potrero Chico** . . . . ☐ **6b**
10m. The right-hand line.

Another three short climbs are located on the small pinnacle in front of the Upper Crag.

③ **Las cosas de Lucas** . . . . ☐ **5** SL TI
10m. The corners on the right-hand side of the face.

④ **Las cosas de Mateo** . . . . ☐ **6a+** TI
10m. The centre of the face.

⑤ **El pilarito** . . . . ☐ **3**
10m. The nicely-positioned arete that faces the valley.

Bolt line but rock dirty

6 Sopo con ondas **6c**
1) 6b, 20m. The left arete of the pillar to a lower-off.
2) 6c, 20m. The upper arete mainly on the left.

7 El beso de la flaca . . . . **5+**
17m. The face to mid-height, past two eyes.

8 Lucky no com pan . . . . . **5+**
17m. The central line up the pillar to the mid-height cave.

9 Danos colaterales . . . . **6c+**
18m. The left-hand continuation of *Lucky no com pan*.

10 Lucas grijander . . . . **7a+**
18m. The right-hand continuation of *Lucky no com pan*.

11 Producto nacional . . . . . **7a+**
35m. A huge pitch up the centre of the pillar passing to the right of the mid-height cave. Slightly eliminate in nature.

12 Filou **6a**
16m. Climb the face past large pockets to mid-height.

13 Forjado en frio . . . . **7b+**
16m. The left-hand line above lower-off of *Filou*.

14 Nunca mais **6c**
16m. The right-hand line above the lower-off of *Filou*.

15 Blanca **6a**
16m. There is a line here but there are no bolts in place.

16 El canalillo de la mari . . **6b+**
33m. The corner is magnificent when dry and clean.

17 Escalopendra guajani **6c**
1) 6b, 16m. Right of corner to a belay/lower-off in a hole.
2) 6c, 18m. The vertical wall above to the top.
Photo on page 82.

18 Zona cero . . . . **7a+**
35m. Huge sustained face in one long pitch.

19 Amor sandunguero **6c**
1) 6c, 15m. The face to mid-height belay or lower-off.
2) 6c, 17m. Continue up the face in the same line.

20 Colaboracion ciudadana . . **7a+**
17m. Thin and perplexing face work.

21 Alta traicion . . . . **7a+**
17m. Similar to *Cloaborcion ciudadana*.

22 Engendro caneri . . . . . . **6a+**
1) 6a, 14m. A nice pitch up slanting cracks.
2) 6a+, 17m. Continue in the same line.

Labels on photo: Upper Crag · Arabesque · The Steps · Sergio · For Fite · Suiza Area · Navegador Pillar

Side tabs: Mijas · Turon · Frontales · Escalera Arabe · Encantadas · The Gorge · Los Cotos · El Polvorin · Makinodromo · Desplomilandia · Abdalajis · El Torcal · V. de Cauche · Archidona · Loja

❶ **Placuneo sin fronteras. .** 🌣 🔲 **7b**
22m. An extremely thin line up a blank looking wall.

❷ **El arabe perdido . . . . . .** 🔲 **7a**
17m. The very thin wall just left of *Bladerunner*.

❸ **Bladerunner . . . .** 🔲 **6a**
17m. The 'elephant's-ear' flake.

❹ **Face of Flake . . . . .** 🔲 **6b**
15m. The front face of the flake.

❺ **Aventur El Chorro . .** 🔲 **7b**
26m. A hard line up the arete right of the corner.

❻ **Lococolo . . . .** 🔲 **7a+**
28m. A very strange line. Does it climb the corner or the face to the right?

❼ **Diedre torpedol . . .** Top L50 🔲 **6c**
26m. A classic and very sustained line that does not let up.

❽ **Arabesque . . . .** 🔲 **7a**
26m. Fine technical climbing up the pillar past a blind pocket.
Photo on page 34.

25 min · Lots of sun · Windy

Sector Arabesque
An attractive pillar of orange-tinted vertical rock that has a couple of the area's best single-pitch lines on it.
Approach - The base of Sector Arabesque is located at the top off the steps.

Mijas · Turon · Frontales · Escalera Arabe · Encantadas · The Gorge · Los Cotos · El Polvorin · Makinodromo · Desplomilandia · Abdalajis · El Torcal · V. de Cauche · Archidona · Loja

Steps Buttress
A compact leaning wall of excellent and well featured rock, located above the steepest section of stone staircase.
Approach - The routes are all started from the steepest section of man made staircase just a little further up the crag base from Sector Sergio.

9 Sheik tu dinero . . . . . . 　　　　　 **6c+**
20m. The left-hand line of the wall is pretty tricky.
Photo on page 85.

10 Birdy . . . . 　　　　 **7b+**
22m. The bulging wall on small holds.

11 Calvo potrun . . . . . 　　　　 **7c**
22m. A bouldery crux but low in the grade and a touch polished.

12 Coming on Strong . . 　　　　 **7a+**
22m. Good wall climbing on hidden holds. Very blind climbing.

13 Rock the Kashbah . . . . . 　　　 **7b**
22m. The right-hand line up tufa and past a low blob.

Mijas | Turon | Frontales | Escalera Arabe | Encantadas | The Gorge | Los Cotos | El Polvorin | Makinodromo | Desplomilandia | Abdalajis | El Torcal | V. de Leuche | Archidona | Loja

La raya

1 Solo afeitar . . . . 🔲 6a
14m. The easy-angled wall to a lower-off is a popular line.

2 The Left Way . . . . 🔲 4+
12m. The left-hand line on the compact triangular slab.
Photo opposite.

3 The Middle Way . . . . . . 🔲 4+
12m. A good if short lived pitch up the middle of the triangular slab.

4 La raya a la izquierda . . 🔲 4
12m. The right-hand line on the triangular slab.

5 Smooth . . . . 🔲 6b+
17m. The smooth slabby wall left of a small left-slanting corner, that looks about 4+!

6 Sergio y Antonio . . . . . . 🔲 6a
30m. An excellent and sustained wall.

7 Yo y mi resaca . . . . 🔲 5+
30m. A fine and clean wall.

8 Blobby Left . . . . 🔲 (6a+)
20m. Climb just left of the prominent tufa blob.

9 Blobby Right . . . . 🔲 (6a)
20m. The wall right of the tufa blob.

10 Chocolate Orange . . . . 🔲 (6a+)
22m. Take on the orange wall and overlap.

The next two routes are on the first section of the cliff reached on the approach path from the road.

11 For Fite . . . . 🔲 6b+
30m. The wall just to the left of a pinnacle leaning up against the base of the cliff. Don't go too direct in the middle section.

12 Double Edge . . . . . 🔲 6b+
30m. Varied climbing up the tall buttress right of a mid-height tree.

Sergio y Antonio

For Fite

Sector Sergio

This area offers a limited but smart mixture of single-pitch easy-angled walls and slabs that are blessed with a stunning outlook.

Approach - The climbs start from an easy-angled approach path that runs up the slope beneath the crag.

Mijas

Tiñon

Frontales

Escalera Arabe

Encantadas

The Gorge

Los Cotos

El Polvorín

Makinodromo

Desplomilandia

Abdalajis

El Torcal

V. de Cauche

Archidona

Loja

Climbers enjoying some late afternoon December sunshine on *The Left Way* (4+) - *opposite* - at Sector Sergio, Escalera Arabe. Photo: Mark Glaister

Short top pitches of *Rogelio* not shown
25 min
Lots of sun
A
A
1
2
3
4
5
6
7
8
9
10
11
12
Chilona

1 Rogelio . . . . Top 50 4+
120m. The easy-angled arete has several short pitches. Abseil back down the line to finish.

2 Chilona . . . . 2 6a+
A popular line with some surprisingly difficult moves. Abseil back down the line to finish.
1) 4, 12m. The easy-angled wall to a ledge.
2) 6a+, 12m. The technical slabby wall proves to be quite tough.
3) 6a, 10m. A steeper pitch to a tree.

3 Tapa de Isabella . . . . (5?)
15m. An unfinished line?

4 O sole mio 1 4
14m. Climb past an overlap to a hidden lower-off left of a tree.

5 Spaguetti Napoletana . . 1 4+
14m. Move right out of *O sole mio* and finish right of the tree.

6 Los timbales . . . . Top 50 4
20m. A long well-travelled line up the middle of the slab.

7 Un helado para Leo 1 3
12m. Start left of small tree/bush.

8 Go on 1 3
12m. Start right of the small tree/bush.

9 El artista 4
12m. An uninspiring short pitch that starts just left of a corner.

10 Dos tetas tiran 2 6b
17m. The steep arete is as good as it appears. High in the grade.

11 Mas que un carreta 1 6a
16m. The wall right of the arete.

12 Three Dishes Menu 1 5
14m. A good wall to a bush.

Highway to Africa
25 min
Lots of sun
A
13
14
15
16
17
18
19
20
La Gaita - 70m

13 Cafe . . . . 5+
15m. Climb the easy-angled arete.

14 Con leche . . . . 5+
15m. The face right of *Cafe*.

15 Highway to Africa 6b
1) 5+, 32m. A worthwhile pitch in its own right.
2) 6b, 20m. A long and sustained pitch.

16 Marlen Suzuky 6c
The harder companion to *Highway to Africa* is also good.
1) 6a+, 32m. A fine sustained wall pitch.
2) 6c, 20m. Another excellent pitch.

17 Los ultimos del ano . . . 6c+
25m. A nice face climb left of a broken corner with a hard move at the top to finish.

18 Yogu con mititilla 6a
10m. The short wall right of broken corner.

19 No hoy trequa . . . . 6a+
10m. A thin hard wall left of tree. *Photo on cover.*

20 Fallilo . . . . 6b+
9m. A thin hard wall left of pinnacle. There may be another short route right of this.

Sector Suiza

A long easy-angled section of the crag that links the main Escalera Arabe area with the Pillar. The crag has plenty of single-pitch climbs in the lower grades spread across three separate developed sections. There are also some popular multi-pitch climbs.
Approach - A good path runs beneath the crag that links the Escalera Arabe area to El Navegador Pillar.

The next climbs are on a wall 70m to the right.

21 Grounded . . . . 4+
30m. The left-hand broken wall only has two bolts.

22 Kiwi 5
22m. The left-most line on the main bolted wall itself.

23 Sorbet de limón . . . . . . 4+
22m. Good sustained climbing.

24 La Gaita . . . . 4+
23m. Lovely long wall up the centre of the wall.

25 Tira-mi-su . . . . 5+
22m. The wall right of a crack, passing a scar.

26 Flan de caramelo 5
21m. A final line up the right-hand side of wall.

La Gaita

El Navegador - 100m

21 22 23 24 25 26

Mijas · Turon · Frontales · Escalera Arabe · Encantadas · The Gorge · Los Cotos · El Polvorin · Makinodromo · Desplomilandia · Abdalajis · El Torcal · V. de Cauche · Archidona · Loja

El Navegador Pillar

The huge soaring pillar visible on the right of the Escalera Arabe has some good mid-grade single-pitch lines, plus an appealing longer route.

Approach - The base of the pillar is reached either via a good path along the base of the cliffs from Sector Suiza, or by walking a little further up the road to a bend below the pillar from where a short path gains the base of the crag.

Lowering-off - Some of these pitches are longer than 30m in length. Take care when lowering off.

❶ **Pecho lobo** 6b
20m. A good starter up the wall just right of a corner to a finish right of a tree.

❷ **Steady Away** . . . . . 6b+
25m. A direct pitch starting just to the left of the ground level cave. *Photo on page 4.*

❸ **Pecho lata** 7a
25m. Pull up through the centre of the cave and make hard moves up the wall to easier ground.

❹ **El Navegador** . . . . .
Opposite.

❺ **Los genelos** 6c
33m. The wall to the left of the hole starting up a flake.
Photo on page 37.

❻ **Los genelos Right** 7a
33m. The line going right of the hole at mid-height.

❼ **La sonrisa vertical** 6c
35m. A fantastic climb that is both sustained and varied.

❽ **Longarone** 6c
35m. The right-hand start allows the meat of *La sonrisa vertical* to be enjoyed again.

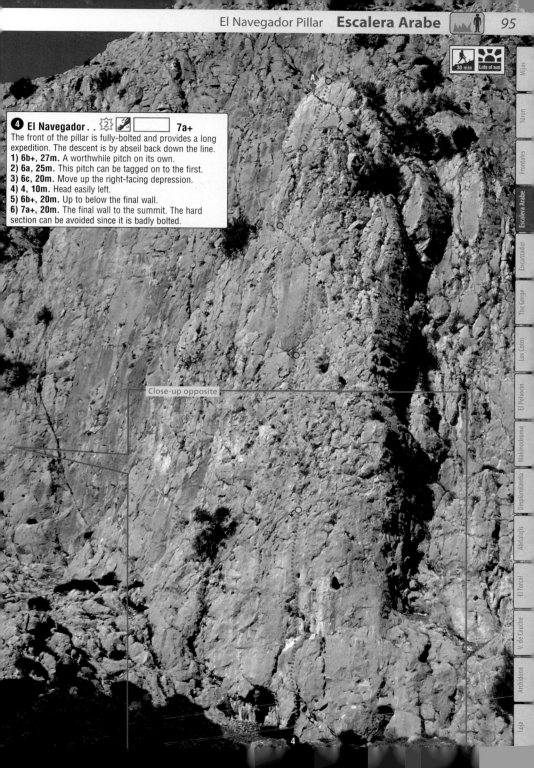

④ El Navegador . . 7a+

The front of the pillar is fully-bolted and provides a long expedition. The descent is by abseil back down the line.

1) 6b+, 27m. A worthwhile pitch on its own.
2) 6a, 25m. This pitch can be tagged on to the first.
3) 6c, 20m. Move up the right-facing depression.
4) 4, 10m. Head easily left.
5) 6b+, 20m. Up to below the final wall.
6) 7a+, 20m. The final wall to the summit. The hard section can be avoided since it is badly bolted.

30 min Lots of sun

A

Close-up opposite

Mijas
Túron
Frontales
Escalera Arabe
Encantadas
The Gorge
Los Cotos
El Polvorín
Makinodromo
Desplomilandia
Abdalajís
El Torcal
V. de Cauche
Archidona
Loja

El Chorro
Las Encantadas

Mijas

Turon

Frontales

Escalera Arabe

Encantadas

The Gorge

Los Cotos

El Polvorin

Makinodroma

Desplomilandia

Abdalajis

El Tortal

V. de Cauche

Archidona

Loja

Mijas

Turon

Frontales

Escalera Arabe

Encantadas

The Gorge

Los Cotos

El Polvorin

Makinodromo

Desplomilandia

Abdalajis

El Torcal

V. de Cauche

Archidona

Loja

The sustained *Chorro mundo* (7a+) - *page 101* - is just one of many fine single-pitch lines at the beautifully located and accessible Las Encantadas, El Chorro. Photo: Mark Glaister

The magnificent cliff of Las Encantadas - *the Enchanted Crag* - lives up to its name. It is set in a commanding position, overlooking the valley that runs down to Málaga, and has a set of routes that deserve the attention of all climbers who enjoy long, sustained and technical wall climbs; the harder routes especially are amongst the best in the area. If the crag has a fault then it is that it catches all the sun that is going and turns into an unbearable oven in warm conditions.

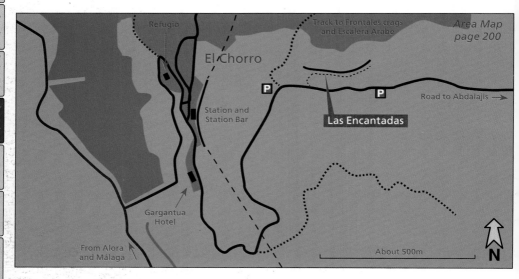

Approach

Las Encantadas is reached from El Chorro village by following the road past the Station Bar and carrying straight on up out of the village on the road to Valle de Abdalajis. After 0.5km the road levels out and the crag comes into view on the left just above the road. On the road directly below the crag are pull-offs on the right - park here and walk back down the road a few metres to below the far left end of the crag. From here pick up a path that heads right to the base of the crag. For the upper crag use the same approach and from the right end of the lower crag walk and scramble up rightwards to the upper crag. Do not approach the crag directly above the building below the crag.

Access

In the past bad behaviour by climbers resulted in the owner banning climbing and removing many of the first bolts, however this situation has now eased and most of the bolts are back in, new routes have started to be put up and some rebolting work undertaken. Nevertheless, good behaviour here is absolutely essential; the owner has the property below the crag and noise should be kept to a minimum and no dogs are permitted.

Conditions

The crag gets the sun for almost all of the day and can be very hot although it does pick up a breeze. The climbs all dry quickly after rainfall but there isn't usually much climbing to be had when it is raining.

Chris Gore pulling through the final bulge on the difficult central line of *Un lait fraiche pour monsieur* (7b) - *page 101* - at Las Encantadas, El Chorro. Photo: Mark Glaister

Mijas
Turon
Frontales
Escalera Arabe
Encantadas
The Gorge
Los Cotos
El Polvorin
Makinodromo
Desplomilandia
Abdalajis
El Torcal
V. de Cauche
Archidona
Loja

The first climb is on an isolated short wall 30m to the left of the main buttress.

1 Bolondro . . . . ✏️ 🪝 [ ] **6a+**
10m. A small amount of gear is required.

2 Nombro propio . . . . ☼ 🪝 ✏️ [ ] **6a**
10m. The pocketed rib just to the right of a tree at the crag base.

3 Bohem destrell . . . . ☼ ✏️ 🪝 [ ] **6a+**
10m. The thin wall to a lower-off under a large nose of rock.

4 Poum, poum, ram, ram . 🪝 ✏️ [ ] **6a**
10m. An old pitch that requires some gear.

5 Para que disfrute la Canalla
. . . . ☼ ✏️ [ ] **6b**
15m. Power up the rounded flake to a rib and follow this to a lower-off.

6 Crisis de identidad . . . . . . ☼ [ ] **6a+**
15m. Take the slanting thin crack to a rib and follow this to the lower-off of *Para que disfrute la Canalla*.

The next route starts just to the right of the large broken corner.

7 The Rib . . . . ☼ [ ] **6a+**
20m. Climb the wide rib.

🏃 3 min | 🐾 Lots of sun

8 Atenea . . . . ☼ ✏️ [ ] **4+**
13m. The easy cracks just right of a tree at the base of the crag.

9 Geisha . . . . [ ] **6a**
14m. Nice climbing all the way. Bolts may be missing.

10 Program genocida . ☼ 🪝 ✏️ [ ] **6b**
17m. This line now goes to the right of its original start and is a bit easier than it used to be.

11 Mañon tropo . . . . . ☼ ✏️ ▯ [ ] **7a+**
22m. The excellent wall to an overhang that is passed with the help of chipped holds above.

12 Por el interes te quiero Andres
. . . . ☼ [ ] **7b**
22m. Climb the wall and pass the high overhang on the right.

13 Las mulas comen muchas cuerdas
. . . . ☼ 🪝 ✏️ [ ] **8a+**
32m. A brilliant climb that needs cool conditions.

14 Un lait fraiche pour monsieur
. . . . ☼ 🪝 ✏️ [ ] **7b**
33m. A precarious and technical start gains easier ground before a steep finishing bulge.
Photo on page 99.

⑮ Generación límite . . . 🔲🔲🔲 **7b+**
35m. A stunning wall pitch.

⑯ Gharanata . . . . 🔲🔲 **8b**
35m. The left-hand side of the peach-coloured streak.

⑰ Mama Endika . . . . . 🔲🔲🔲 **8a+**
35m. The impressive and gradually steepening wall.

⑱ Last Minute . . . . 🔲🔲 **7a**
24m. The wall left of the corner.

⑲ Bueno, bonito y barato
🔲🔲🔲 **6c+**
26m. The bulging rib right of the wide crack is not quite as difficult as it first appears.

⑳ Chorro mundo . . . . 🔲🔲🔲 **7a+**
25m. The wall, crack and overhang are a popular challenge.
Photo on page 96.

㉑ La ley del Cateto . . . . . 🔲🔲 **6c+**
24m. A magnificent and sustained pitch that follows the long open groove.

The next two routes are around 20m to the right of La ley del Cateto and are not shown on the topo.

㉒ Mataillos lugareños . . . 🔲🔲 **6c**
16m. The pocketed wall is well worth hunting down.

㉓ Artemisa . . . . 🔲🔲🔲 **5+**
13m. The well-defined short arete is also worthwhile.

Las Encantadas

The crag is split into two sections, the lower left-hand side is a large wide wall whilst the upper wall on the right is a tall vertical wall of excellent red rock.
The first bolts on many of the climbs were removed but most have now been replaced. Some routes still need a wire or two but there is new bolting taking place so the situation may change. To be on the safe side, bring some wires with you.
Access - Keep the noise level down, park carefully and strictly no dogs are allowed at the crag.
Approach - From the parking directly below the crag locate a steep approach path that starts to the left of the crag when facing it.

Lowering-off - Some of these pitches are longer than 30m in length. Take care when lowering off.

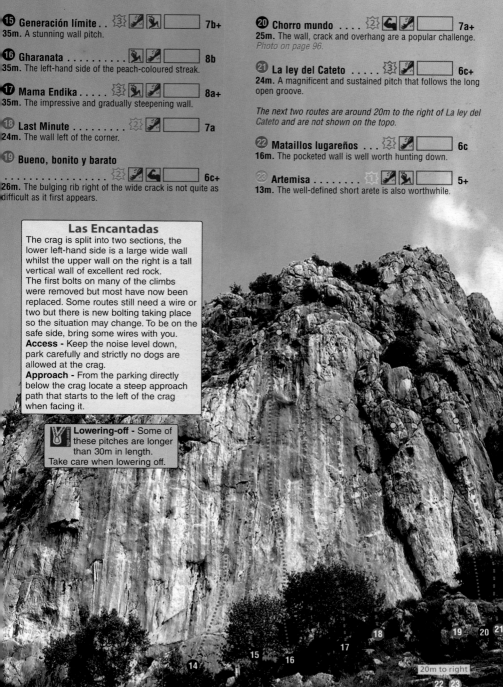

20m to right

Side tabs: Mijas · Túron · Frontales · Escalera Árabe · Encantadas · The Gorge · Los Gotos · El Polvorin · Makinodromo · Desplomilandia · Abdalajis · El Torcal · V. de Couche · Archidona · Loja

Las Encantadas - Upper

A very good crag with some of the best hard routes in the area. The climbs are all sustained, on superb rock, and get lots of sun. The crag is a real sun-trap. There is not usually any dry climbing in the rain on this sector.
Approach - From the main crag walk right and up for 50m to the base of the wall.

❶ Tipo indio . . . . 7b+
26m. The steep left-hand side of the gully

❷ No me miras mal 8a
27m. The right wall of the gully.

❸ No puedo controlarme . . . . . 6c+
15m. Short but thin and technical climbing up the wall at the base of the gully.

❹ Espoloa nombrada . . . . 7a+
15m. A puzzling and fingery little number.

The next routes require a long rope to lower-off safely.

❺ Un poco vicioso . . . . . . 7a+
30m. Climb to the bulge high up, starting from a high ledge.

❻ Mezcla explosiva 8a
35m. The long and blank left-hand wall past a bolt-on hold.

❼ Kit grimpe 7c
28m. A wall climb past a bolt-on hold.

❽ Gros rouge 7b
28m. A thin lower wall, left of a large flake at 9m, gains the steeper well-featured upper section. *Photo opposite.*

❾ Redders 7a
30m. A superb pitch.

❿ Sara . . . . 7a+
30m. A sustained and beautiful climb.

⓫ Bailando con osos 7b
30m. Weave your way up the front of a pillar.

⓬ Dura vida la de un frekee
. . . . 6c+
30m. A nasty start is followed by superb climbing that leads to a fluttery finish.

⓭ Fiebra de sur 7a
30m. Branch right from *Dura vida la de un frekee.*

Mijas

Turon

Frontales

Escalera Arabe

Encantadas

The Gorge

Los Cotos

El Polvorín

Makinodromo

Desplomilandia

Abdalajís

El Torcal

V. de Cauche

Archidona

Loja

Dan Arkle executing the upper sequence of moves on *Gros rouge* (7b) - *opposite* - on the Upper Wall at Las Encantadas, El Chorro. Photo: Mark Glaister

Mijas

Turon

Frontales

Escalera Árabe

Encantadas

The Gorge

Los Cotos

El Polvorin

Makinodromo

Desplomilandia

Abdalajis

El Torcal

V. de Cauche

Archidona

Loja

El Chorro
The Gorge

A party enjoying the classic multi-pitch route *Zeppelin* (6c+) - *page 119* - in The Gorge. Photo: Mark Glaister

Mijas

Túron

Frontales

Escalera Arabe

Encantadas

The Gorge

Los Cotos

El Polvorin

Makinodromo

Desplomilandia

Abdalajís

El Torcal

V. de Cauche

Archidona

Loja

Mijas

Turon

Frontales

Escalera Arabe

Encantadas

The Gorge

Los Cotos

El Polvorin

Makinodromo

Desplomilandia

Abdalajis

El Torcal

V. de Cauche

Archidona

Loja

Main photo: the tunnel above Sector Africa in flood. Photo: Chris Dainton
Above: the entrance to The Gorge. Photo: Mark Glaister

The massive defile of El Chorro's signature feature 'The Gorge' is one of Andalucia's most famous landmarks, made all the more significant by the Walkway (or Camino del Rey - *King's Path*); the narrow man-made walkway that clings to the walls of The Gorge. The Walkway was built in around 1905 to enable access and inspection to the workings in The Gorge and named after the visit of King Alfonso XIII in around 1921. Over the years the Walkway has fallen into disrepair and some sections have disappeared or been removed. For climbers the Walkway has become one of the great attractions of El Chorro since it offers an atmospheric approach to many of the routes, and adds dizzying exposure to the climbing right from the first move. Despite these attractions, the climbing focus in El Chorro has moved away from The Gorge in recent years and many of the routes are becoming neglected although the best climbs still see ascents, especially in hot weather. The two big multi-pitch classics of *Africa* and *Zeppelin* remain as popular as they have ever been.

Conditions

The climbs on Los Venenos and Santimonia get plenty of sun and can become unbearably hot but are pleasant first thing in the morning. El Recodo and the sectors deep within the walls of The Gorge are good spots to head for when it is hot offering shady climbing, often with a pleasant cooling breeze. This same cooling breeze can make these sectors unbearably cold at other times. Very occasionally the water levels in the river and the tunnels rise and prevent access to the Africa Wall also making the river crossing impossible. Climbing is possible in light rain on some of the faces, and in heavy rain on the steeper routes in El Recodo.

The Gorge, Los Cotos, El Polvorin and the Makinodromo Area are best approached by the Walkway. This has undergone some radical changes that have now left it in a more user-friendly state. The initial 25m of the Walkway has been dismantled and a via ferrata of sorts constructed that allows easy access (easy for climbers) to the Walkway. With a harness and slings it is straightforward to self-protect the via ferrata by clipping into the numerous bolts and rungs. The Walkway itself is slowly deteriorating but now this also has a series of wires all the way along it that allow a via ferrata style approach. This means that passage of the Walkway is now as fast and probably safer than it has been for many years.

❶ Camino del Rey ...... 〔≶〕 🗗 [＿＿＿] **Grade 1**
The traverse of the whole of the King's Way is a classic trip and, despite the low grade, many folks fail to onsight it!

Approach via the Walkway

Follow the road uphill past the El Chorro Refugio and take the first left at a sharp bend. Follow the road past the entrance to the campsite and along the side of the lake until the road turns inland and a huge railway bridge comes in to view - park on the left. Walk up the higher track above the gated road (the gated road leads directly on from the parking) that climbs to a point that overlooks The Gorge entrance, Green Bridge and railway entrance tunnel (this is where the guards are usually positioned). From here, drop down to some tall railings and traverse left on the outside, above a culvert, to where they end. Then go down left of the bridge to a scree slope that leads to the start of the via ferrata. Using this approach avoids the need to cross any of the rail tracks or the Green Bridge). The Walkway can then be used to access all the sectors in The Gorge. It is also possible to pass through The Gorge, drop down and cross the river to access Los Cotos or El Polvorin.

The Railway Tunnels

Traditionally people used the railway tunnels to approach the Central Gorge area for the crags like Los Cotos and Makinodromo. Access via the tunnels is now illegal and if caught you will get a large fine. At weekends and during public holidays guards police the entrance to the tunnel at the Green Bridge. Additionally, a lot of high fencing has been erected and the traditional entrance to the tunnels at the Albercones parking area is no longer accessible. The good news is that all the climbs can still be reached without entering the tunnels although it requires a little more effort.

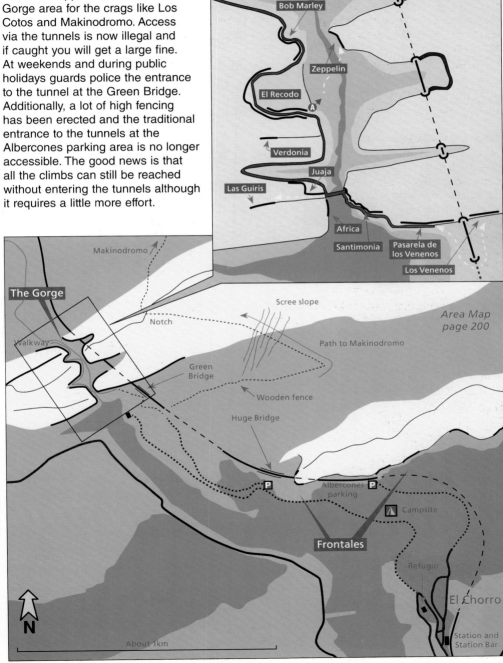

N

Approach to central crags

To Los Cotos and Makinodromo

Bob Marley

Zeppelin

El Recodo

A

Verdonia

Juaja

Las Guiris

Africa

Santimonia

Pasarela de los Venenos

Los Venenos

Makinodromo

Scree slope

Area Map page 200

The Gorge

Notch

Path to Makinodromo

Walkway

Green Bridge

Wooden fence

Huge Bridge

P

Albercones parking

P

Campsite

Frontales

Refugio

El Chorro

Station and Station Bar

N

About 1km

Mijas · Turon · Frontales · Escalera Arabe · Encantadas · The Gorge · Los Cotos · El Polvorin · Makinodromo · Desplomilandia · Ahdalalis · El Torcal · V. de Gaucho

Pasarela de los Venenos

The smooth, vertical wall at the mouth of The Gorge is crossed by the start of the Walkway. All of the routes on this section of the cliff start either under, or off, the Walkway, and are all technical and fingery.

Approach (see page 108) - The Walkway is reached by ascending a via ferrata.

1 Diedro de Hercules . . . . 🖉 ▭ **6b+**
60m. An old route. Start by scrambling down the slope to a ledge with a wire rail just above the waterline. **1) 6b+, 2) 6b.**

2 Luz verde . . . . 🔆🖉 ▭ **7b**
24m. The wall and arete left of the steep section of the via ferrata

3 La cupla la tiene el bar de Isabel ▭ **7a**
11m. Start below a thin roof. Abseil in from Walkway.

4 Fruto prohibido . . . . . . 🪧🪧 ▭ **8b**
23m. Old bolts. Abseil in from the Walkway.

5 Valla plan . . . . 🪧🪧 ▭ **6c+**
20m. Old bolts and rarely climbed. Abseil in from the Walkway.

6 Arco de Goliath . . . 🔆🖉🪧 ▭ **7c+**
30m. Left of the curving arch.

7 Ace ventura . . . . . . 🔆🖉🪧 ▭ **8a**
30m. A good wall climb best left for cool conditions.

8 El ultimo rayo del sol . . 🔆🖉 ▭ **7a+**
26m. Tough climbing. Start from the left side of the low overhang.

9 Ventura con dos tacones 🔆🪧 ▭ **7b+**
20m. A line of newer bolts below the missing Walkway.

10 Ventura con bragus mojadas
. . . . 🔆🪧🪧 ▭ **7a+**
15m. The right-hand line of bolts on the lower wall.

The rest of the routes are accessed from the Walkway.

11 Aixa matinae . . . . 🪧 ▭ **7c+**
10m. The last move requires a dynamic approach.

12 Les cutres . . . . 🔆🪧 ▭ **6b+**
12m. The short leftwards rising line.

13 Demócratas y cristianos
. . . . 🔆🪧🖉 ▭ **7a+**
23m. The right-facing corner.

14 No seas pesada nena 🔆🪧🖉 ▭ **6c+**
23m. A hard start leads to a good groove.

15 Camino Shuffle. 🔆🪧🖉🪧 ▭ **7b**
23m. A technical wall.

Los Venenos

Abseil point to ground at end of the Walkway

Sector Santamonia

Path from Green Bridge

Line of via ferrata access to Walkway

12 min / To mid afternoon

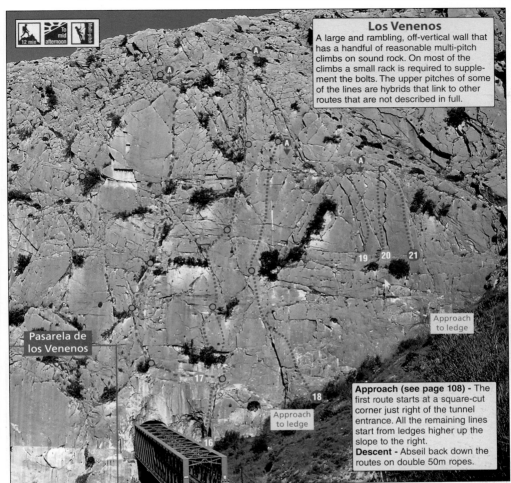

Los Venenos

A large and rambling, off-vertical wall that has a handful of reasonable multi-pitch climbs on sound rock. On most of the climbs a small rack is required to supplement the bolts. The upper pitches of some of the lines are hybrids that link to other routes that are not described in full.

Pasarela de los Venenos

19 20 21

Approach to ledge

Approach to ledge

Approach (see page 108) - The first route starts at a square-cut corner just right of the tunnel entrance. All the remaining lines start from ledges higher up the slope to the right.
Descent - Abseil back down the routes on double 50m ropes.

16 El techito del pirata. 　　　　　　6a
A hybrid line with a smart initial pitch. A rack is needed for the first and last pitches.
1) 6a, 15m. Climb the corner right of the bridge to a ledge.
2) 5+, 12m. Continue direct up to a small tree and then climb up corners to another ledge. Alternatively, climb over a bulge onto a slab on the right and continue direct at **6b+**.
3) 5+, 15m. Move up the wall and then right to a belay.
4) and 5) 5+, 40m. Continue in two long pitches, past occasional fixed gear.

The next route starts from a large ledge up and right of the bridge which is easily gained via ledges from right, or via the first pitch of El techito del pirata.

17 La ampola . . . . 　　　　　　6a
1) 5, 12m. Traverse leftwards over the tunnel to a belay.
2) 6a, 3) 6a, 4) 6a. Climb the wall above in two short pitches and one long pitch. There is a left-hand variation finish at **5+, 5+.**

18 Octopus dei . . . . . . 　　　　　　6c
A sustained and interesting climb up the centre of the wall. Start right of the easy access ledges that lead to the start of *La ampola*.
1) 6c, 28m. Move up the easy wall to some new and old bolts at a smooth wall. Climb the wall, then move left and up to a belay between a large metal spike and bushes.
2) 6a, 28m. Move up and follow the line of bolts just left of a narrow white streak.

To get to the starts of the next three routes, scramble first left then back right to a ledge left of the corner.

19 Victima de la evidence . 　　　　　　6a
10m. A short pitch from the left-hand end of the ledge.

20 Empotrador atómico . . . 　　　　　　5+
12m. The wall left of the corner.

21 Zapatillas jebe . . . . 　　　　　　7a
10m. Start up the corner then move left on to a technical slab.

Reinforcements placed to protect the Walkway from rockfall!

Sector Santimonia

This sector was one of the first sections of The Gorge to be developed but it is now very quiet and some of the routes are becoming a bit neglected with ageing bolts. The best routes though are technical and finger-tweaking walls with masses of exposure. The wall gets the early sun and also picks up a breeze.
Approach (see page 108) - Gain the Walkway using the via ferrata. Follow the Walkway up steps to the first routes that rise above a gap.

❶ Ventana en el tropico . . . . . 7a+
10m. A short problematic pitch above the Pipe Bridge.

❷ Camino sin ander . . . . 6a+
On the far side of a big gap in the Walkway is this long route. The pitch grades are **1) 4, 2) 6a, 3) 6a+, 4) 4.**

❸ Sendero luminoso 6b
A long mixed expedition that starts at the base of The Gorge with a hard aid pitch. Access by abseil.
1) 5+/A2, 2) 6a, 3) 3. The starting pitches.
4) 6b. The pitch above the Walkway is rather unappealing.
5) 6a+. The continuation above.
Descent - Lower off pitch 4 or abseil from higher up.

❹ Polva de angel . . . . 8b?
17m. A hard line through the roof is a bit of an enigma.

❺ Hartelo 7b
23m. The hanging arete with lots of exposure.

6 Sangre latina . . . . 🔲 6c
26m. The stunning central corner is high in the grade.

7 La tregua del pedal. 🔲 7c+
28m. The towering wall has a scrappy start. The last move can be out flanked on the left at **7c**.

8 Santimonia . . . . 🔲 6c+
The best of the routes on this sector with three varied and interesting pitches and with the added bonus of good rock.
1) 6c+, 16m. The left-hand crack is an excellent pitch.
2) 6a, 20m. The middle pitch leads to a belay below a ledge, and is harder if taken direct.
3) 6b+, 15m. The last pitch gives more finger-crack climbing.
Descent - Abseil off.

9 Desos de domino 🔲 7a+
16m. The right-hand of the two cracks.

10 Jabega . . . . 🔲 7b+
16m. The blank wall and small overlap is chipped.

11 Moco de hierro . . . . . . 🔲 6c
12m. A short route with a tricky start.

The next routes are approached by abseil from the Walkway.

12 Libertad de movimiento 🔲 7a+
Abseil from the far side of the bridge. The easy first pitch is used to access the 7a+ pitch. The pitch grades are **1) 3, 2) 7a+**.

13 Lobo de mar . . . . 🔲 7a+
26m. A tough pitch.

14 Moudjaidine . . . . 🔲 6c
17m. A short pitch which has been rebolted.

15 Chupa la gamba . . . . . . 🔲 6c
A run-out route. Access by abseil.
1) 6c. Exciting! Make sure you are confident at 6c before attempting this pitch.
2) 6b. The well-positioned arete.

Jauja

16 Enimigo público . . . . 🔲 7b+
14m. Step out left from the Pipe Bridge and climb up to, and through, a desperate finishing roof.

17 Jauja . . . . 🔲 7a+
18m. The blank wall gets progressively harder with height.

18 E por doquier . . . . 🔲 8a+
18m. The very thin grey wall left of a crack.

19 Granainos '85 . . . . 🔲 6b
28m. Start as for *E por doquier* but move right to the steep crack. Large gear is needed for the crack.

20 Atlética y llorica . . . . 🔲 7b
28m. The wall right of the crack.

Las Guiris

Jauja

Approach scramble to sector Las Guiris

21 Una española nunca mea sola
. . . . 🔲 7b+
30m. A little further along the Walkway is a fine clean wall that gives good, sustained wall climbing.

Las Guiris
Approach by an awkward and precarious scramble (grade 3) up banking where a large cable is attached.

22 Lefty . . . . 🔲 7c
15m. Short wall on the left.

23 Page Maker . . . . 🔲 7b+
17m. The right-hand bolt line.

24 Cangreo . . . . . . 🔲 8c+
30m. The left-hand line on the fine streaked wall.

25 Monsters Forever 🔲 8b
30m. The right-hand line has the same start as *Cangreo*.

Sector Jauja and Las Guiris
The two sectors offer hard wall climbing. Although both were forcing grounds in their day the routes now see little traffic. The walls are generally shady but do get sun late in the day. Both sectors can be breezy at times.
Approach (see page 108) - Gain the Walkway using the via ferrata. Follow the Walkway across the Pipe Bridge and Sector Jauja is immediately on the left. Sector Las Guiris is set up high on the rim of the gorge above the Walkway.

Mijas · Turon · Frontales · Escalera Arabe · Encantadas · The Gorge · Los Cotos · El Polvorin · Makinodromo · Desplomilandia · Abdalajis · El Torcal · V. de Cauche · Archidona

Africa Wall

Directly opposite Sector Santimonia is an enormous wall cut with vertical crack systems that point dizzyingly to the narrow strip of water at the bottom of The Gorge. This is the Africa Wall - a huge wilderness where it is easy to get lost! The climbs have a big feel about them and a full rack is required, even though some of the routes are bolted.

Approach (see page 108) - Gain the Walkway using the via ferrata. Follow the Walkway across the Pipe Bridge to Sector Jauja. The Africa routes start from the lowest ledge at the base of the wall. This is reached by crawling along a short tunnel that starts at the base of Sector Jauja. At the tunnel's end, make a 52m abseil (exciting) to a ledge, which is 30m above the water. From here, traverse leftwards across the wall to belays. If the initial pitch of *Africa* looks wet it is easy to gain the stance at the top of the first pitch by climbing easily up left to an abseil point and then making a leftward trending abseil to the stance (see topo). On rare occasions the access tunnel is water filled and the approach is impassable.

Descent - Traverse rightwards along one of the ledge systems and abseil, or scramble, back to the tunnel entrance. If you are unfortunate enough to have failed before you have got above the tunnel entrance, then you will have to abseil into the river and swim for it. This is not recommended as anything other than a good story to tell your friends.

The first three routes start at a the left-hand end of the ledge. Traverse left past a bolted belay and around a rib to a peg belay in a crack.

❶ Material belico

.... 🔲🔲🔲🔲⬜ **6a**

Follow the crack and corner system to the left of the belay. The climbing is straightforward but there is not a lot of fixed gear to point the way. Take a full rack including some large stuff. There is a curious lower pitch at A2, which presumably starts from a boat. The pitch grades are **1) 4, 2) 5, 3) 5, 4) 6a.**

❷ Africa ..... 🔲🔲🔲⬜ **6b+**

The classic route of the wall follows a series of excellent grooves and cracks. *Photo opposite.*
1) 6a+, 2) 6b+. Two well-bolted pitches gain the mid-height ledge system.
3) 5, 4) 6b+. There is a hard direct finish to the right of the last pitch at **7a+.**

❸ La bella y la bestia

.... 🔲🔲🔲⬜ **7a+**

A hard and sustained route which starts as for *Africa*, then continues straight up the wall above. The line is well bolted but take a small rack just in case. Pitch grades - **1) 6a+, 2) 7a+, 3) 7a, 4) 7a.**

Mijas
Turon
Frontales
Escalera Arabe
Encantadas
The Gorge
Los Cotos
El Polvorin
Makinodromo
Decplomilandia
Abdalajis
El Torcal
V. de Cauche
Archidona
Loja

The next three routes start from the bolted belay at the base of the approach abseil.

4 Chiripitiglauticos 6b+

A variation on *Africa*. The line goes up leftwards to the first belay on *Africa*. From here it wanders up the wall on the right, eventually finishing up the last pitch of *Africa*. Take a full rack of gear.
Pitch grades are **1) 5+, 2) 6a, 3) 5+, 4) 6b+**.

5 La dame del viento 7a

A magnificent route up the right-hand side of the wall. Mostly bolted but take some wires for the start of pitch one.
1) 6c, 2) 6c. Climb direct to the mid-height ledge.
3) 6b+, 4) 7a. Two long crack systems lead to a final pitch up the headwall.

6 Cuando se lo diga a mis amigos 6c+

This route takes a direct line up the wall, starting up *La dame del viento*. Take a full rack.
1) 6c. As for *La dame del viento*.
2) 6b, 3) 6c+, 4) 6b+. Three pitches up the crack system on the right-hand side of the wall.

15 min | Early morning | multi-pitch | Windy

The stunning position on the second pitch of *Africa* (6b+) - *opposite*. Climbers: Dan Arkle and Neil Morbey. Photo: Mark Glaister

Verdonia

A wall of good rock perched high up above the Walkway but with only three lines on it. High up and exposed, receives early sun.

Approach - Start from the Walkway and use the route *Verdonia* to access the upper three routes.

1 Verdonia . . . . ☐ **5**
An access route to the upper wall. Pitch grades - **1) 5, 2) 5.**

2 Moloko plus . . . . ☐ **6c+**
25m. The highest of the bolted lines.

3 Enano pagano . . . . ☐ **6c+**
25m. The right-hand bolted line.

4 Harte drogadisto . . . . ☐ **5+**
25m. A semi-bolted line.

El Recodo

5 Pixci . . . . ☐ **6b+**
10m. A micro line at the far left end of some high ledges.

6 Dixci . . . . ☐ **6c+**
10m. The harder sister route to *Pixci.*

7 La canastera . . . . . ☐ **7b+**
27m. A brilliant wall climb which would be worth three stars if it were not escapable.

8 Sangre nueva . . . . ☐ **7a**
30m. The narrow corner, starting up *Canastera.*

9 Tipo sueca . . . . ☐ **7a**
30m. A stunning wall climb with a hard move low down and a tricky finish. High in the grade.

10 Calígula . . . . ☐ **7b+**
The superb second pitch is worth seeking out.
1) 6c, 16m. Climb the shallow corner groove to a hanging belay at the prominent hole, or continue.....
2) 7b+, 14m. Excellent moves up the arete and right wall.

11 El campista . . . . . . ☐ **7b+**
22m. Thin and insecure moves via the slim groove.

12 Musas inquietantes ☐ **8a**
22m. Magnificent climbing that is sustained and very fingery.

13 Todos pretenden saber . ☐ **6c+**
10m. Abseil off bolts behind the Walkway, below and left of *Pixci.*

There are some interesting routes starting from the hanging gardens below the Walkway. Access to the base is via iron rungs or an abseil from the Walkway.

14 Los gozas y las sombras ☐ **7a**
Abseil in from anchors on the far left. This is the abseil to reach the gorge bottom to access *Zeppelin (page 119).*
The pitch grades are **1) 6c+, 2) 7a.**

15 King Kong . . . . ☐ **6b+**
16m. Start at a bolt belay and finish up a hard crack.

16 Indio jumeli . . . . ☐ **6c**
16m. The start is hard and below the first bolt - take care!

17 El Recodo . . . . ☐ **6a+**
16m. The unspectacular route which gives the sector its name.

18 Six Vicious . . . . ☐ **6b+**
16m. The rightward-facing corner.

19 Tu misimo . . . . ☐ **7a+**
16m. The hard blank wall.

20 Sietebe del plumero ☐ **7b+**
15m. Hard and cruxy!

21 Miss dedos . . . . ☐ **6c+**
15m. Start below a hole.

22 Cachito . . . . ☐ **6c**
16m. The left-hand line on the orange wall.

23 Nachito . . . . ☐ **6b**
16m. The right-hand line on the orange wall.

El Recodo

El Recodo

This superb and atmospheric wall gives the most developed climbing in The Gorge. It is usually quiet but can be busy during the local holidays. It is also a total 'shade-trap' and can be cold although there is shelter from the Gorge wind. Climbing in the rain is possible.

Approach (see page 108) - Gain the Walkway using the via ferrata. Follow the Walkway across the Pipe Bridge and continue over a small bridge across a huge gap (scary!) and then on around the corner to the steep secluded sector.

20 min | Not much sun | Sheltered

Access from Walkway down iron rungs

Mijas
Turon
Frontales
Escalera Arabe
Enkantadas
The Gorge
Los Cotos
El Polvorin
Makinodromo
Desghanilandia
Abdalajis
El Torcal
V. de Cauche
Archidona
Loja

El Recodo - Right

The steep right-hand side of this sector has some good routes and one infamous long stamina pitch.

❹ Apache . . . . 　　7a+
A long two pitch route up steepening ground right of the cave. The pitch grades are 1) 6b, 2) 7a+.

❺ Lluvias otoñales . . . . 　　5+
28m. A line below the Walkway. Abseil from two bolts.

Bob Marley Area

❻ Epi y blas . . . . 　　5+
24m. The first line just around the arete from *El Recodo*.

❼ La musa chica . . . . 　　6c
24m. A well-positioned blank grey wall.

❽ Rasta de posta . . . . . . 　　6b+
24m. High in the grade.

❾ Come unas . . . . 　　6a+
24m. The last of the quartet on this section of wall.

There are reported to be some single-pitch lines under the Walkway but no details are known.

❿ Bob Marley . . . . . . 　　7c
20m. Superb and technical, but short-lived.

⓫ Los capitalistas . . . . . 　　7c+
18m. A desperate fingery route up the blank wall.

⓬ Rovicunda . . . . 　　6b
18m. Fun climbing up and around the cave.

⓭ Haale bop . . . . 　　6a+
18m. The right edge of the corner/cave is a pleasant pitch.

⓮ Maestro Golpeador . . . . 　　6b
22m. Below the Walkway. Abseil from the start of *Haale Bop*.

❶ Iriquieza . . . . 　　7c+
1) 7b+, 18m. The well-chalked flake is popular and pretty tough.
2) 7c+, 25m. The extension is less well travelled.

❷ Hari-kiri. . . . . 　　8c+
45m. A mere 8c, 8a+ if you split it at a hanging stance. There is a project start to the right which joins at the mid-height lower-off.

❸ Bon Voyage . . . . 　　6c
An excellent route up the right-hand side of the cave.
1) 6c, 22m. Start up steepening rock from the right edge of cave.
2) 6b+, 25m. Continue up the steep line above the belay.

Bob Marley Area

A little frequented section of the crag although only a short hop from El Recodo. The routes are on good rock. It can be cold here especially if a wind is blowing. Climbing in light rain is possible.
Approach - Continue along the Walkway from El Recodo.

Sector Zeppelin

The largest section of wall in The Gorge is opposite El Recodo. The most obvious features of the cliff are the line of three massive caves, Los Tres Techos, and to their left a huge wall and ridge of great rock. The area around the Tres Techos Caves has a number of slightly gloomy hard pitches and some big aid lines (not described), whilst the wall to the left holds the major multi-pitch classic *Zeppelin*.

Approach - Follow the Walkway to El Recodo and, from the lower sector, abseil down the line of *Los Gozas y las sombras* (page 116) to the base of The Gorge and cross the river via the huge boulders. Check the water level before abseiling in. This approach avoids the need to enter the tunnels.

Descent

Approach across river

🔟 Zeppelin

Top 50 6c+

This El Chorro classic is a superb long climb. The route is well equipped but take a small rack to supplement the fixed gear. Pitches 4 and 5, which are much harder than the others, can be climbed using some aid. Start at the base of the long slab which leads up to the prominent roof. *Photo on page 104.*

1) 4+, 20m. Climb the slab to a belay at some trees.
2) 6a+, 25m. Continue up the pleasant slab to a bush.
3) 5+, 25m. Climb up more slabs to a stance under the prominent roof.
4) 6c, 20m. The roof is overcome by an exciting and strenuous traverse to a hanging stance on the lip.
5) 6c+, 25m. Hard moves above the stance lead left to easier climbing back right above. Don't go too far left. Worth 7a if combined with the previous pitch since the belay becomes a point of aid.
6) 5+, 30m. Follow the right-trending crack up the slab - spaced bolts.
7) 6b+, 25m. Follow the crack in the groove above then move right and up onto the ridge.
8) 3, 40m. Scramble easily rightwards along the ridge to belay behind a tree on the right.
9) 6b, 35m. Climb the corner to the top of a pinnacle then continue up the wall above.
10) 65m. Scramble up the left-hand side of the ridge.
Descent - Scramble left down a large terrace, below some large caves, back down to the railway line.

There are a few hard routes on the steep lower wall.

⓫ Mar de Venus

8c

20m. Start up the slope.

⓬ Shaka zulu

8b

20m. The well-chalked line.

⓭ Perspectiva neiwski

8b+

20m. Follow the vague arete.

⓮ Gresca gitana

8a+

20m. The right-hand line.

30 min | To mid afternoon | Windy

Mijas
Turón
Frontales
Escalera Arabe
Encantadas
The Gorge
Los Cotos
El Polvorin
Makinodromo
Desplomilandia
Abdalajis
El Torcal
V. de Cauche
Archidona
Loja

Mijas

Turon

Frontales

Escalera Arabe

Encantadas

The Gorge

Los Cotos

El Polvorin

Makinodromo

Desplomilandia

Abdalajís

El Torcal

V. de Cauche

Archidona

Loja

The slabby walls of Los Cotos hold numerous single-pitch classics. Pictured here is *Number One* (4+) - *page 126* - at Los Cotos Medios. Photo: Mark Glaister

El Chorro
Los Cotos

Mijas

Turón

Frontales

Escalera Árabe

Encantadas

The Gorge

Los Cotos

El Polvorín

Makinodromo

Desplomilandia

Abdalajís

El Torcal

V. de Cauche

Archidona

Loja

The slabs of smooth and subtly-featured limestone that make up Los Cotos are a welcome alternative to the steep and strenuous climbs on the neighbouring cliffs that surround it. The setting in the secluded central Gorge area is magnificent, making it a lovely place to enjoy some fine climbing with the sun on your back, but best avoided in warm weather.

Los Cotos was one of the first places to be developed for sport climbing at El Chorro and the style and grades are considered by many to be a little 'old school'. A few of the lines have been upgraded to bring them in line with the routes elsewhere and some gear has been replaced, but there are still a number of routes which require a small rack to supplement the sparse fixed gear. For those who want to get the most out of the place, taking a few wires is a good idea. Cotos Medios is the most frequented section whilst Cotos Altos has the best lines and rock. Cotos Bajas is set down next to the river and is a lovely spot but the routes are not as good and much of the gear is in need of an update. In warm conditions the polish on the popular lines makes itself well felt although it has got no worse over the last decade or so.

Approach

Los Cotos is best approached through The Gorge although traditionally most people have used the now-banned tunnels. The details of the approach from the village and passage along the Walkway through The Gorge are on page 108. Once through The Gorge, continue along the Walkway until a path leads down to the orange groves and river. Cross the river and walk a short way to Cotos Bajas and further on under the railway to the Medios and Altos areas.

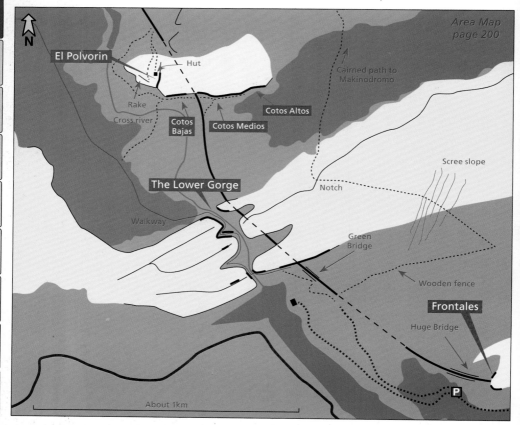

Conditions

Los Cotos is a huge sun-trap getting the sun from first thing in the morning until late afternoon although there is plenty of shade available at the base of the crags from bushes. The more popular climbs are polished and are best avoided in humid and hot conditions. The crag is especially well sheltered from cold northerlies but is best avoided in the wet.

Perfect winter weather and rock on the classic *Super galleta* (6a) - *page 126* - one of many intense and challenging wall and slab climbs at Los Cotos, El Chorro. Photo: Mark Glaister

Mijas · Turon · Frontales · Escalera Arabe · Encantadas · The Gorge · **Los Cotos** · El Polvorin · Makinodromo · Desplomilandia · Abdalajis · El Torcal · V. de Cauche · Archidona · Loja

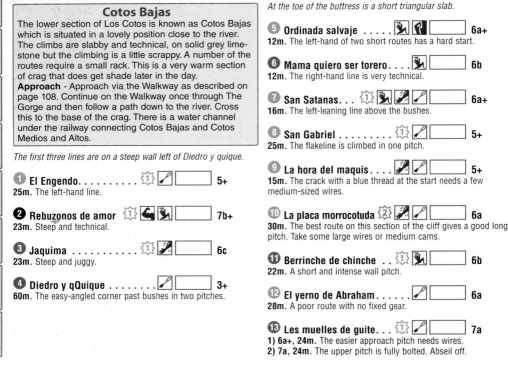

Cotos Bajas

The lower section of Los Cotos is known as Cotos Bajas which is situated in a lovely position close to the river. The climbs are slabby and technical, on solid grey limestone but the climbing is a little scrappy. A number of the routes require a small rack. This is a very warm section of crag that does get shade later in the day.

Approach - Approach via the Walkway as described on page 108. Continue on the Walkway once through The Gorge and then follow a path down to the river. Cross this to the base of the crag. There is a water channel under the railway connecting Cotos Bajas and Cotos Medios and Altos.

The first three lines are on a steep wall left of Diedro y quique.

1 El Engendo. . . . . 5+
25m. The left-hand line.

2 Rebuzonos de amor 7b+
23m. Steep and technical.

3 Jaquima 6c
23m. Steep and juggy.

4 Diedro y qQuique . . . . 3+
60m. The easy-angled corner past bushes in two pitches.

At the toe of the buttress is a short triangular slab.

5 Ordinada salvaje . . . . . 6a+
12m. The left-hand of two short routes has a hard start.

6 Mama quiero ser torero. . . . 6b
12m. The right-hand line is very technical.

7 San Satanas. . . 6a+
16m. The left-leaning line above the bushes.

8 San Gabriel . . . . 5+
25m. The flakeline is climbed in one pitch.

9 La hora del maquis. . . . 5+
15m. The crack with a blue thread at the start needs a few medium-sized wires.

10 La placa morrocotuda 6a
30m. The best route on this section of the cliff gives a good long pitch. Take some large wires or medium cams.

11 Berrinche de chinche . . 6b
22m. A short and intense wall pitch.

12 El yerno de Abraham. 6a
28m. A poor route with no fixed gear.

13 Les muelles de guite. . . 7a
1) 6a+, 24m. The easier approach pitch needs wires.
2) 7a, 24m. The upper pitch is fully bolted. Abseil off.

Cotos Medios - Left

The first routes on the magnificent Cotos Medios are on the slightly more broken section of crag, just right of the tunnel entrance. This is an extremely hot spot getting all the sun that is going.

Approach - Approach via the Walkway as described on page 108. Continue on the Walkway once through The Gorge and then follow a path down to the river. Cross this to the base of Cotos Bajas. Walk up through the water channel under the railway to Cotos Medios.

⑭ **Camella cojo** . . . . 🔆📏⬜ 5
25m. Climb a crack past one bolt to a lower-off at a tree.

⑮ **Fisuroterapia** . . . . . 🔆2️⃣📏⬜ 5
28m. A good and popular crack pitch starting past some bolts. Gear is needed for the crack.

⑯ **Fisura de los Santos** 1️⃣🔆📏⬜ 5
28m. A worthwhile right-hand alternative to *Fisuroterapia*.

⑰ **Fisura de hombre** . . . . . 2️⃣🔆⬜ 5+
30m. A cracking pitch which sadly has old gear.

⑱ **Bitchitos on the Wailers** . . . 🔧⬜ 5
20m. The bulge is tough.

⑲ **El Monstruo de las galletas**
. . . . 1️⃣🔆🔆⬜ 5+
28m. The centre of the long sustained slab.

⑳ **Mordiscos de amor** . . . . 🔆📏⬜ 5
28m. Start from a higher vegetated ledge.

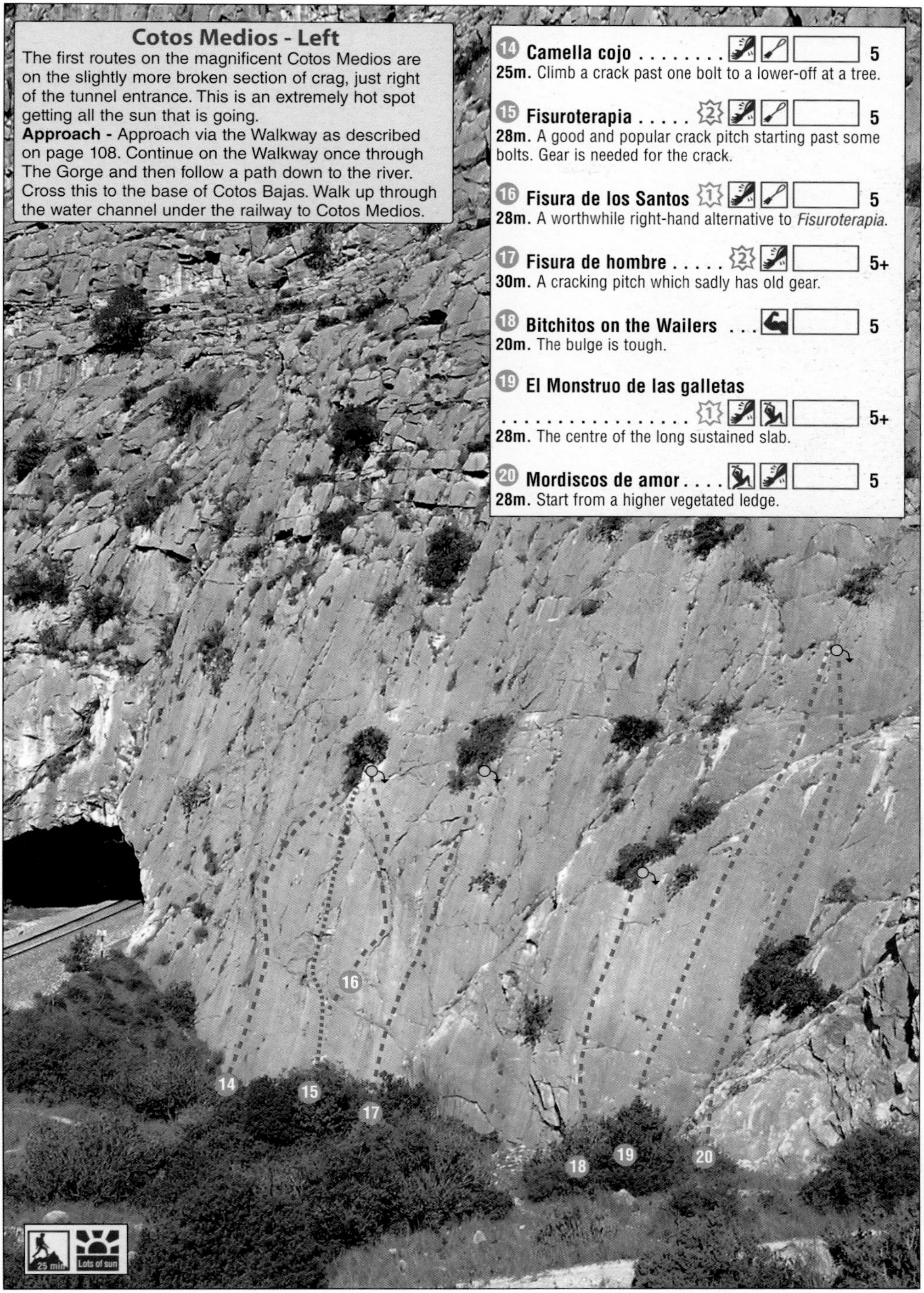

Mijas
Turon
Frontales
Escalera Arabe
Encantadas
The Gorge
Los Cotos
El Polvorin
Makinodromo
Desplomilandia
Abdalajis
El Torcal
V. de Cauche
Archidona
Loja

16

14   15

17

18   19   20

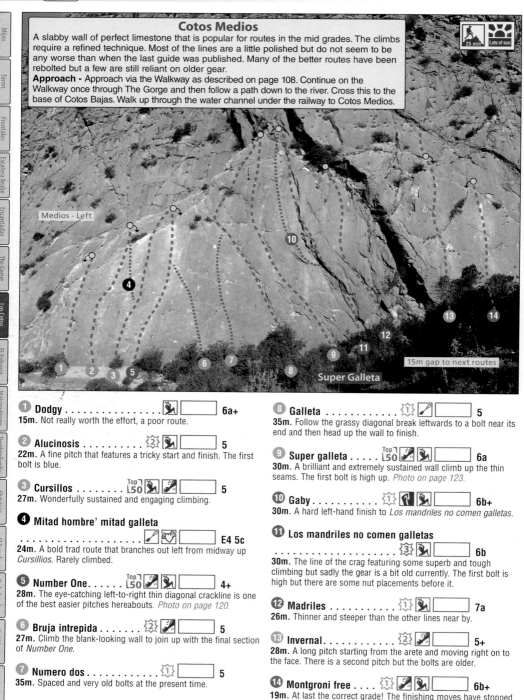

Cotos Medios

A slabby wall of perfect limestone that is popular for routes in the mid grades. The climbs require a refined technique. Most of the lines are a little polished but do not seem to be any worse than when the last guide was published. Many of the better routes have been rebolted but a few are still reliant on older gear.

Approach - Approach via the Walkway as described on page 108. Continue on the Walkway once through The Gorge and then follow a path down to the river. Cross this to the base of Cotos Bajas. Walk up through the water channel under the railway to Cotos Medios.

Medios - Left

Super Galleta

15m gap to next routes

---

1 Dodgy . . . . 6a+
15m. Not really worth the effort, a poor route.

2 Alucinosis 5
22m. A fine pitch that features a tricky start and finish. The first bolt is blue.

3 Cursillos 5
27m. Wonderfully sustained and engaging climbing.

4 Mitad hombre' mitad galleta
. . . . E4 5c
24m. A bold trad route that branches out left from midway up *Cursillios*. Rarely climbed.

5 Number One . . . . . . 4+
28m. The eye-catching left-to-right thin diagonal crackline is one of the best easier pitches hereabouts. *Photo on page 120.*

6 Bruja intrepida 5
27m. Climb the blank-looking wall to join up with the final section of *Number One*.

7 Numero dos 5
35m. Spaced and very old bolts at the present time.

8 Galleta 5
35m. Follow the grassy diagonal break leftwards to a bolt near its end and then head up the wall to finish.

9 Super galleta 6a
30m. A brilliant and extremely sustained wall climb up the thin seams. The first bolt is high up. *Photo on page 123.*

10 Gaby . . . . 6b+
30m. A hard left-hand finish to *Los mandriles no comen galletas*.

11 Los mandriles no comen galletas
. . . . 6b
30m. The line of the crag featuring some superb and tough climbing but sadly the gear is a bit old currently. The first bolt is high but there are some nut placements before it.

12 Madriles 7a
26m. Thinner and steeper than the other lines near by.

13 Invernal . . . . 5+
28m. A long pitch starting from the arete and moving right on to the face. There is a second pitch but the bolts are older.

14 Montgroni free . . . . 6b+
19m. At last the correct grade! The finishing moves have stopped many 5+ leaders.

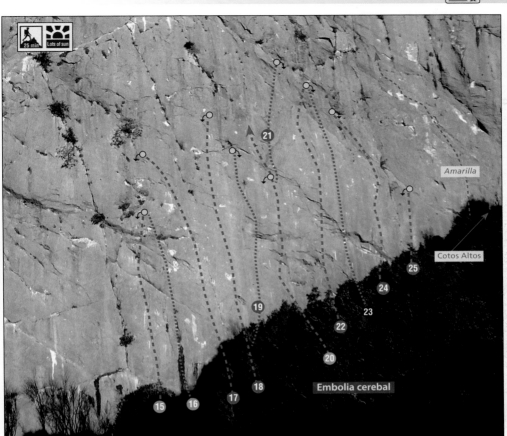

Mijas

Turon

Frontales

Escalera Arabe

Encantadas

The Gorge

Los Cotos

El Polvorin

Makinodromo

Desplomilandia

Abdalajis

El Torcal

V. de Cauche

Archidona

Loja

Amarilla

Cotos Altos

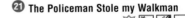

Embolia cerebral

---

15 Cebolla pa la olla . . . . . 6a+
13m. The left-hand line of thin cracks to a lower-off.

16 Genesis . . . . 6a+
13m. The line of thin cracks just right of *Cebolla pa la olla*.

17 Arbola 6b
20m. A highly technical thin crack that requires some care getting to the first bolt.

18 Bruner and the Bruna 6b
25m. Gain a small round pocket at 7m and continue up the thin wall that gradually eases as height is gained. Old bolts.

19 La ley de la selva . . . . . 6b+
25m. Start as for *Bruner and the Bruna* but follow the line of green-painted bolts past a rockover move on the upper wall.

20 Embolia cerebral . . 5+
25m. An all out friction move gains better holds and the first bolt. Continue to double bolts and abseil. The gear on the old top pitch seems to have gone, or the line may continue from what is now the lower-off of *La ley de la selva*.

21 The Policeman Stole my Walkman
. . . . 6b
32m. The line continuing rightwards from the lower-off on *Embolia Cerebral* is worthwhile and best done in a single-pitch.

22 Güirilandia 7a
25m. The very thin line just right of *The Policeman Stole my Walkman*.

23 Cafe bonk . . . . 7a+
25m. More extremely technical and thin wall work..

24 Penetración analgésica
. . . . 6c
25m. The rounded, right-trending corner is a superb but tough exercise. The lower-off is a long way to the left.

25 Si te caes pega una voz 6c
9m. Short and desperate. Only one bolt long.

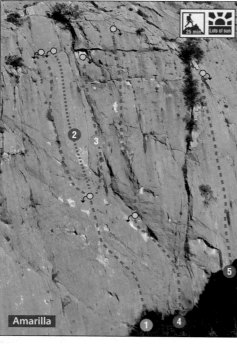

Amarilla

Mijas
Turon
Frontales
Escalera Árabe
Encantadas
The Gorge
Los Cotos
El Polvorín
Makinodromo
Desplomilandia
Abdalajís
El Torcal
V. de Cauche
Archidona
Loja

Cotos Altos

The upper area of slabs is the most extensive section of the cliff with a number of good but hard pitches which will suit those who like a good fight at the grade. Cotos Altos is much less frequented than the neighbouring Cotos Medios. It is a very warm spot that does go into the shade later in the day.

Approach - Approach via the Walkway as described on page 108. Continue on the Walkway once through The Gorge and then follow a path down to the river. Cross this to the base of Cotos Bajas. Walk up through the water channel under the railway to Cotos Medios. The path up to the start of Cotos Altos is good but becomes difficult to follow towards the upper routes and is best taken on the opposite side of the hillside from the crag.

❶ Amarilla . . . . 5+
1) 5, 25m. Looks to be harder than grade 5 climbing.
2) 5+, 25m. Wires needed for this pitch.

❷ Fanáticos del atico
. . . . 6c
25m. The fully-bolted central variation pitch 2 to *Amarilla*.

❸ El ventorro . . . . 6a+
25m. The right-hand variation pitch 2 to *Amarilla*. This climb can also be started up *La blanca*.

The upper section of the crag is to the right of a prominent left-to-right slanting break. The first route starts below and left of this.

❹ La blanca 6b
1) 5, 20m. Climb up to the break and move leftwards to a belay.
2) 6b, 25m. Climb through the bulge above the stance to a wall.

❺ Guerrero del abismo
. . . . 7a
30m. A superb slab climb up the smoothest section of the crag.

❻ Exceso de equipaje . 6c
30m. The crack requires wires.

❼ Chungo superior 6a
1) 5+, 15m. Start just left of a boulder and climb the crack.
2) 6a, 25m. The line directly above the stance.

❽ Quasimodo . . . . . . 7a+
15m. The right-hand branch of the crack provides a testing alternative. A bolt may be missing on the crux.

❾ Profanes y blasfemos 6b+
27m. A good pitch that starts between some boulders.

❿ Pisto gilguero . . . . 6c+
18m. A short and technical crack to easier ground.

⓫ Que te den por culo 6b
1) 6b, 20m. A steep start to easier ground and stance.
2) 5, 26m. The roof on its left needs wires.

⓬ El dinamitate te espera 6c
1) 6b, 20m. The first pitch of *Que te den por culo*.
2) 6c, 25m. Take the right-hand line on bolts through the roof.

⓭ Yu yu 6c
30m. Start up a curving slim groove/crack. **6a** on the right.

⓮ Chulo de madriza 7a
9m. A very short and hard line.

⓯ El piqui 6c
30m. A desperate start - use some blocks.

⓰ Petamorfosis 7b
30m. A good right-hand finish to *El piqui*.

⓱ Mister Proper . . . . 5+
30m. A two pitch semi-trad route with well-spaced bolts. The pitch grades are **1) 5+, 2) 4+**.

⓲ El viajero amable . . 6b+
22m. The thin and sustained slab above the start of *Mister Proper*.

⓳ Adeli . . . . 6b+
22m. The steep slab to the same lower-off as *El viajero amable*.

⓴ Electro Volt . . . . 6b+
22m. The curving corner groove succumbs to bridging.

㉑ Exodo . . . . 6a+
18m. The slim corner. Can be started on the left at **7b+**.

El viajero amable

Guerrero del abismo

Mijas

Túron

Frontales

Escalera Árabe

Encantadas

The Gorge

Los Cotos

El Polvorín

Makinodromo

Desplomilandia

Abdalajís

El Torcal

V. de Cauche

Archidona

Loja

El Chorro
El Polvorin

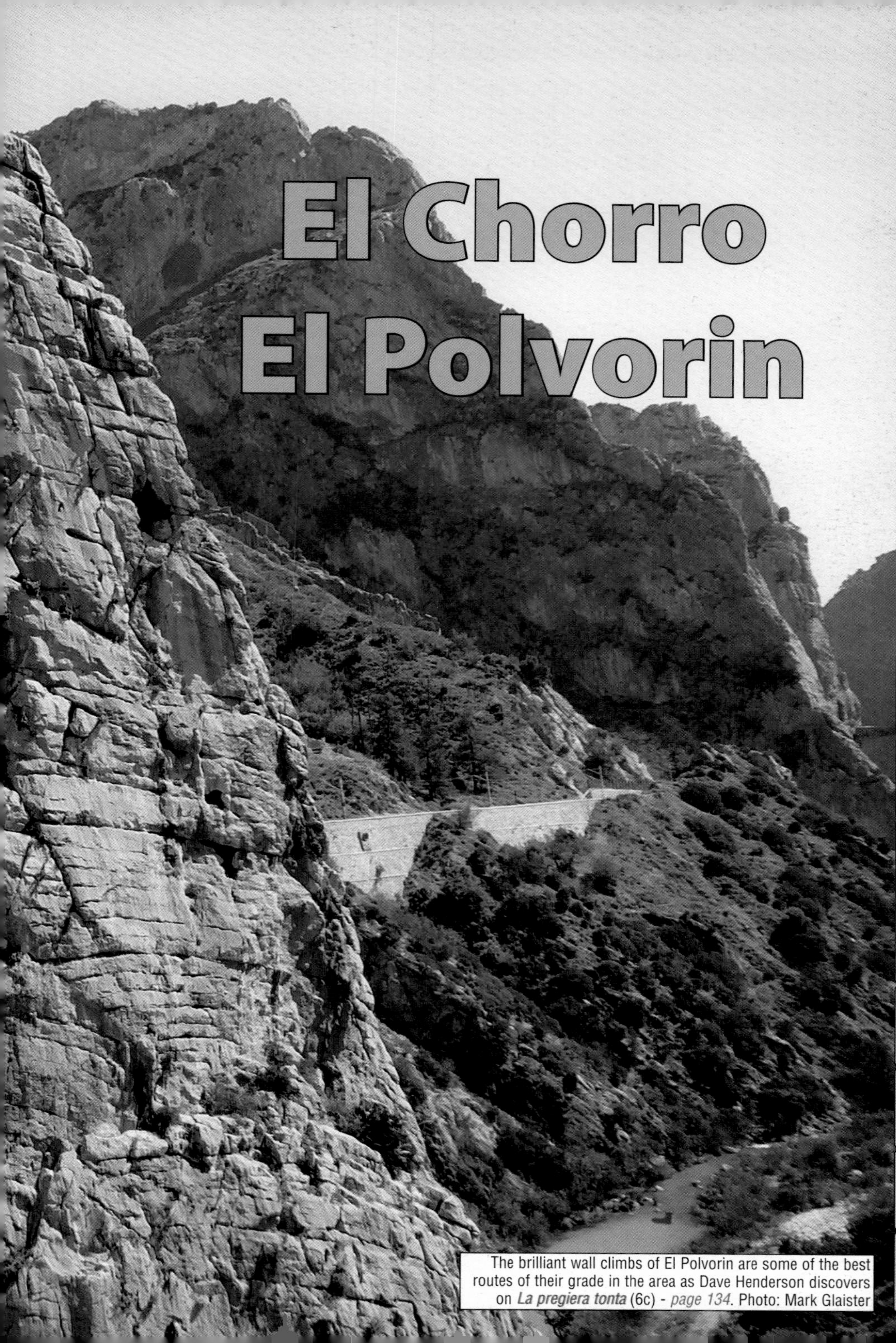

Mijas

Túron

Frontales

Escalera Arabe

Encantadas

The Gorge

Los Cotos

El Polvorin

Makinodromo

Desplomilandia

Abdalajis

El Torcal

V. de Cauche

Archidona

Loja

The brilliant wall climbs of El Polvorin are some of the best routes of their grade in the area as Dave Henderson discovers on *La pregiera tonta* (6c) - *page 134*. Photo: Mark Glaister

Tucked away just out of sight of those travelling along most of the footpaths in the Gorge is El Polvorin, one of El Chorro's premier cliffs. El Polvorin (*the gunpowder magazine*) is named after the small hut on its flank that presumably housed the explosives used to excavate the railway tunnels, however the routes on the crag itself have more of slowburn rather than explosive character about them. Indeed, for those looking for sustained mid-grade wall pitches, there are few places with such quality climbs as those on offer here.

On first inspection from the convenient viewing ledge, the wall would appear to be heavily featured and well supplied with horizontal breaks, cracks and lots of good pockets but, once embarked on, the features become hidden from view and evermore tiring progress has to be made in the belief that something will come to hand.

The rock is immaculate and the bolts are in good condition but at times feel a bit spaced. As a consequence this is not a place to venture if unfit. Many of the climbs are now bolted to a height of 35m so that they may be climbed and lowered on a single 70m rope. Intermediate lower-offs are in place on the cliff to aid descent for those with shorter ropes or, alternatively, descent can be made by abseil from the top of the crag, or by carefully scrambling off leftwards.

Approach

The approach to El Polvorin is a little complicated when you avoid using the tunnels. Follow the Walkway approach as described on page 108. Once through The Gorge, continue along the Walkway until a path leads down to the orange groves and river. Cross the river and scramble steeply up a ramp to a viewpoint below the wall. Alternatively, take an easier but slightly longer path on the left, up to the railway line and then head back to the cliff on a good path that leads quickly to a viewpoint that overlooks the crag. This path splits and the upper path goes to the small hut and the lower to the viewpoint. From the viewpoint an exposed scramble gains the base of the crag.

Conditions

The cliff faces west getting the afternoon sun. In cool or windy weather it is best avoided until the sun gets on to the main face. In warm weather the main face soon heats up and has no shade at the base. There is no possibility of climbing in the rain.

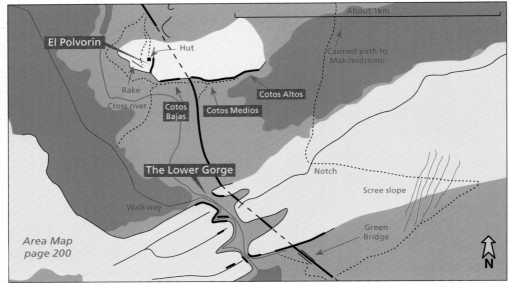

El Polvorin — Hut — Cairned path to Makinodromo — About 1km — Rake — Cross river — Cotos Bajas — Cotos Medios — Cotos Altos — The Lower Gorge — Notch — Scree slope — Walkway — Green Bridge — Area Map page 200 — N

Mijas

Turon

Frontales

Escalera Arabe

Encantadas

The Gorge

Los Cotos

El Polvorin

Makinodromo

Desplomilandia

Abdalajis

El Torcal

V. de Cauche

Archidona

Loja

Unlocking the technical sequence midway up the *Pilier dorada* (6c) - *page 134* - at El Polvorin, El Chorro. Photo: Dave Henderson (Glaister Collection)

El Polvorin

El Polvorin is one of El Chorro's best crags. The climbs stand shoulder to shoulder with the best of their style anywhere and a visit should not be missed. Since the last guidebook there has been a lot of rebolting work on the main section of the wall that has also involved the rationalizing and slight realignment of some of the lines. Along with the rebolting of the lines has been the addition of more lower-offs that allow the routes on the main face to be climbed in massive single pitches.

Approach - Carefully scramble from the viewing area across to the crag. Particular care is needed for the routes which start further down the slope.

Up and left of the main face is a small hut that is useful as a landmark for the first two routes that are not of the same quality as the other routes on the cliff but are at easier grades.

① El gordo ya no come guarro . . . ☐ **5+**
15m. Start by the little hut.

② Pedro el grande . . . . ☐ **6a**
20m. The grey wall 30m to the right.

Routes from Alerta roja to Los crocodrilos no lloran start from the large sloping ledge beneath the face that is gained via a scramble either from above, or by traversing in at the level of the ledge.

③ Alerta roja . . . . . . ☐ **6b+**
32m. Start at the first line of bolts just right of the base of the corner/gully. A fine technically sustained line which is just a bit close to the gully at the bottom.

④ Sueño de Venus . . . . . . ☐ **6a+**
32m. An outstanding expedition which gains a long line of good holds, after a tricky start as for *Alerta roja*. An excellent introduction to the wall.

⑤ Pilier dorada . . . . ☐ **6c**
32m. The 'Golden Pillar' is an extremely fine pitch with sustained and varied climbing plus a couple of hard moves thrown in. Start up a wide break and continue to an easing before taking on the subtle pillar and steep ground above. *Photo on pages 15 and 133.*

⑥ Generación spontanea
. . . . ☐ **6c**
32m. A huge line with little respite. Climb the wall to a large cave. Exit this via a fingery move to some pumpy ground above. *Photo on page 6.*

⑦ Revuelta en el frenopático
. . . . ☐ **6c+**
32m. The thin blank wall direct between the holes.

⑧ Habitos de un perturbado irrediable
. . . . ☐ **6c**
35m. A great climb offering continually interesting climbing from start to finish. A good rest can be had in the mid-height cave. Probably as good as the two other Top 50 routes above.

⑨ La pregiera tonta . . ☐ **6c**
32m. Yet another masterpiece with the difficulties confined to the lower two thirds of the pitch. *Photo on page 130.*

⑩ Games moya . . . . ☐ **6a+**
15m. An easier start to *La pregiera tonta.*

The next lines from Obsesion permanente to Los crocodrilos no lloran start at various belay points located on the slightly loose slope below the wall. TAKE GREAT CARE WHEN DESCENDING THIS SLOPE.

⑪ Obsesion permanente . . ☐ **6c**
38m. A superb route which can be split at a small stance.

⑫ Araña mecánica . . . . . . ☐ **6b+**
20m. A short route to the third stance of *Paca eugene.*

⑬ Nirvana . . . . ☐ **6b+**
1) 5, **15m.** Climb up the crack to a ledge.
2) 6b+, **26m.** Fine climbing on the upper wall.

⑭ Romo y extraploma. . . ☐ **6c**
26m. Starting from the belay at the top of pitch 1 of *Nirvana*, climb the wall to the right.

⑮ Urbi et orbe . . . . ☐ **7a**
12m. Very artificial and escapable.

⑯ Los crocodrilos no lloran ☐ **7a+**
15m. Slightly better than its left-hand sister.

The next route can be reached from above by locating a scree rake about 120m left of the crag (looking in) and descending this back in the direction of the crag to river level. Alternatively the start can be accessed by walking around from the base of Cotos Bajas - see page 124.

⑰ Paco Eugene . . . . . ☐ **6a**
A long and classic expedition. Start at the base of the face. The lower two pitches need a small rack. If you wish to do the upper section of the route only, it can be reached via pitch 1 of *Nirvana*.
1) 5, **18m.** Climb the wall past some bolts. Wires needed.
2) 4, **23m.** Continue up the easiest line to a large belay ledge. Wires needed.
3) 5, **10m.** Climb up leftward to the start a crack system.
4) 6a, **20m.** The crack to the top.

Lowering-off and Descent - Most of the major routes are equipped with lower-offs at 32m. For those who do not have a 70m rope there are intermediate lower-offs at convenient points on the face. It is also easy to traverse off along the top of the crag. There is also an abseil point for those who have double ropes.

70m rope required
to lower-off

A Abseil Point

Mijas

Tiron

Frontales

Escalera Arabe

Encantadas

The Gorge

Los Cotos

El Polvorin

Makinodromo

Desplomilandia

Abdalajis

El Torcal

V. de Cauche

Archidona

Loja

Mijas
Turon
Frontales
Escalera Arabe
Encantadas
The Gorge
Los Cotos
El Polvorin
Makinodromo
Desplomilandia
Aldalajis
El Torcal
V. de Cauche
Archidona
Loja

El Chorro
Makinodromo

Mijas

Turon

Frontales

Escalera Árabe

Encantadas

The Gorge

Los Cotos

El Polvorín

Makinodromo

Desplomilandia

Abdalajís

El Torcal

V. de Cuorhe

Archidona

Loja

A climber above the first section of *Life is Sweet* (6c) - *page 146* - at Makinodromo, El Chorro. Photo: Mark Glaister

The reputation of El Chorro as a destination for sport climbing is mainly built upon the notoriety of the truly awesome section of cliff known as Makinodromo, and in particular the central line up its largest and most severely overhanging wall of tufa - *Lourdes*. A couple of decades on since its first ascent, *Lourdes* is still one of the most famous climbs in the World and many come to El Chorro only to try this one route! Today *Lourdes* has been joined by dozens more climbs on the Makinodromo itself, and also the whole of the long line of cliff that the Makinodromo is just one part of. This new development still has a long way to go, but the climbs on areas like Los Tigres are a promising pointer to the quality of routes that still remain to be discovered. The development of these cliffs is ongoing so there are quite a lot of projects and odd bolts dotted about which can cause some difficulty when identifying routes, although the best and most popular lines are always very well chalked up. The climbing in this area is really the preserve of those operating in the higher 'black spot' grades although a good day can be had for those wanting to pick off the better mid-grade 'red spot' routes, culminating in the outstanding *Life is Sweet*.

Approach

The Gorge Approach -
Follow the Walkway through the gorge (see page 108) and continue on the other side until you can pick up a path down to the river. Cross the river then walk leftwards under El Polvorin and follow a path up to the railway. Cross this and head up the slope past a small hut taking the best line for the desired area - see map.

The Notch Approach -
From the path that looks down on the Green Bridge continue up the path (that has a wooden handrail) until a flat area is reached. Head right up the line of a scree slope and then cut back left along a faint path towards a notch on the ridge and cross here. Once on the other side a faint cairned path leads across the hillside to the Life is Sweet area. This long walk is superb with magnificent views and probably takes about the same time as The Gorge Approach.

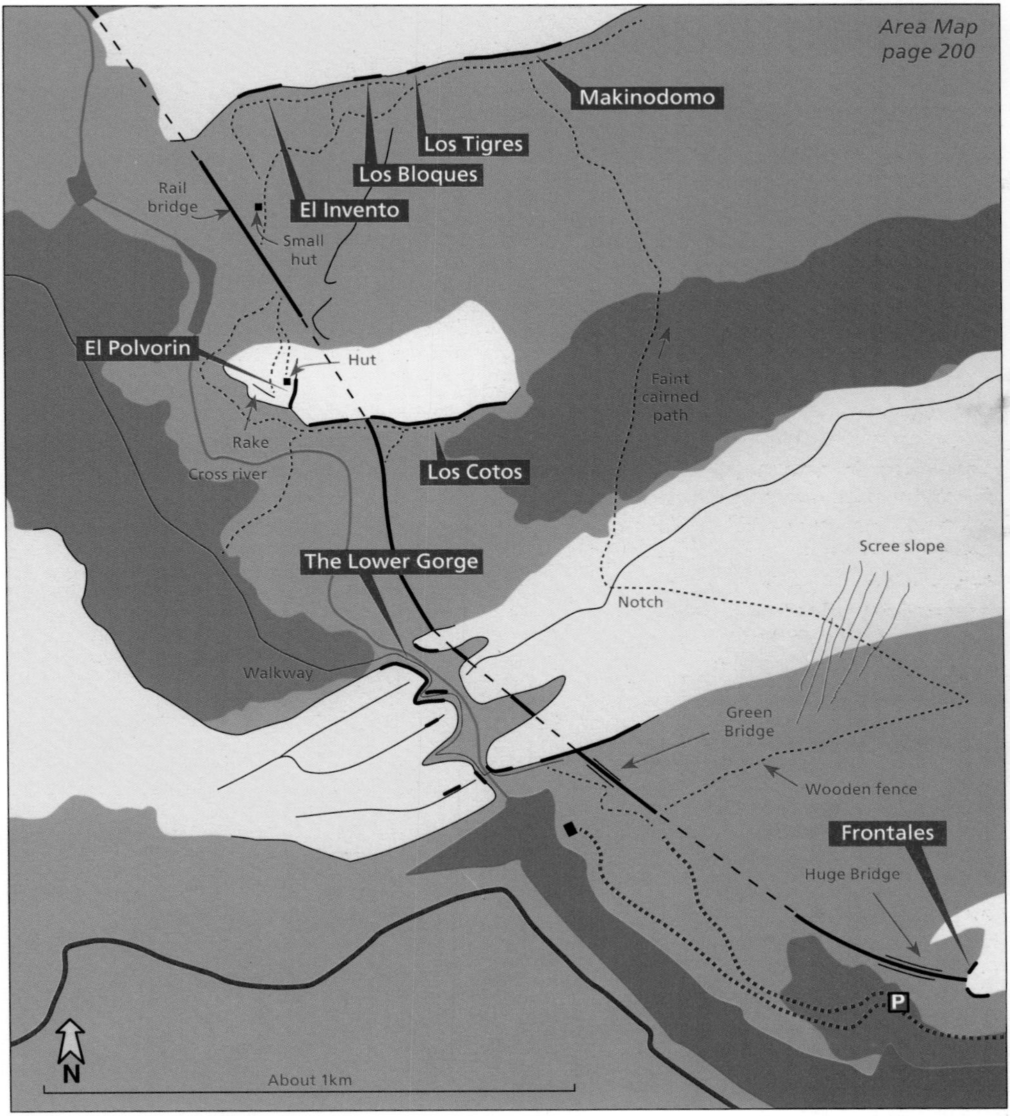

Area Map page 200

Makinodomo

Los Tigres

Los Bloques

El Invento

Rail bridge

Small hut

El Polvorin

Hut

Los Cotos

Rake

Cross river

The Lower Gorge

Faint cairned path

Scree slope

Notch

Walkway

Green Bridge

Wooden fence

Frontales

Huge Bridge

P

N

About 1km

Mijas | Turon | Frontales | Escalera Arabe | Encantadas | The Gorge | Los Cotos | El Polvorin | Makinodromo | Desplomilandia | Abdalajis | El Torcal | V. de Cauche | Archidona | Loja

Conditions

The whole of the escarpment faces south and gets the sun for most of the day, dipping into the shade late in the day. As a consequence it is often very warm although the area does sometimes catch a breeze. Outside of the winter months when the sun is high in the sky the steepest parts of the cliff are in the shade for much longer. Climbing in the rain is most definitely an option although the tufas start to seep after prolonged spells of rainfall. There are a number of trees at the base of the crag that offer shade but there is no water source.

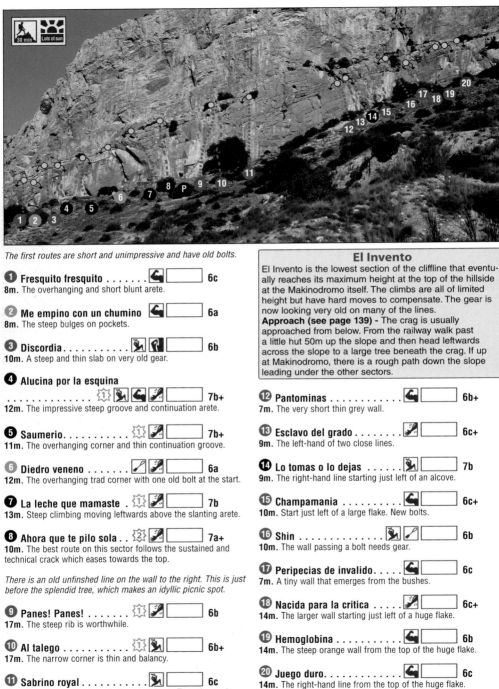

The first routes are short and unimpressive and have old bolts.

❶ Fresquito fresquito 6c
8m. The overhanging and short blunt arete.

❷ Me empino con un chumino 6a
8m. The steep bulges on pockets.

❸ Discordia 6b
10m. A steep and thin slab on very old gear.

❹ Alucina por la esquina
. . . . 7b+
12m. The impressive steep groove and continuation arete.

❺ Saumerio . . . . 7b+
11m. The overhanging corner and thin continuation groove.

❻ Diedro veneno 6a
12m. The overhanging trad corner with one old bolt at the start.

❼ La leche que mamaste . 7b
13m. Steep climbing moving leftwards above the slanting arete.

❽ Ahora que te pilo sola . . 7a+
10m. The best route on this sector follows the sustained and technical crack which eases towards the top.

There is an old unfinshed line on the wall to the right. This is just before the splendid tree, which makes an idyllic picnic spot.

❾ Panes! Panes! 6b
17m. The steep rib is worthwhile.

❿ Al talego . . . . 6b+
17m. The narrow corner is thin and balancy.

⓫ Sabrino royal 6c
15m. A hard start and not much easier above. Treat the grade with caution.

El Invento
El Invento is the lowest section of the cliffline that eventually reaches its maximum height at the top of the hillside at the Makinodromo itself. The climbs are all of limited height but have hard moves to compensate. The gear is now looking very old on many of the lines.
Approach (see page 139) - The crag is usually approached from below. From the railway walk past a little hut 50m up the slope and then head leftwards across the slope to a large tree beneath the crag. If up at Makinodromo, there is a rough path down the slope leading under the other sectors.

⓬ Pantominas . . . . 6b+
7m. The very short thin grey wall.

⓭ Esclavo del grado . . . . 6c+
9m. The left-hand of two close lines.

⓮ Lo tomas o lo dejas 7b
9m. The right-hand line starting just left of an alcove.

⓯ Champamania . . . . 6c+
10m. Start just left of a large flake. New bolts.

⓰ Shin 6b
10m. The wall passing a bolt needs gear.

⓱ Peripecias de invalido 6c
7m. A tiny wall that emerges from the bushes.

⓲ Nacida para la critica . . . . . 6c+
14m. The larger wall starting just left of a huge flake.

⓳ Hemoglobina 6b
14m. The steep orange wall from the top of the huge flake.

⓴ Juego duro 6c
14m. The right-hand line from the top of the huge flake.

Los Bloques

Further up the hill from El Invento is an area where some huge blocks have fallen away from the main face. This is Los Bloques, a complex area with a few short technical routes, and a couple of longer offerings. This isn't a great area but it is worth a look if you are passing.

Approach (see page 139) - The crag is usually approached from below. From the railway, walk past a little hut 50m up the slope and continue up a good path that gradually heads leftwards to the cliff where a scramble over boulders gains the base. It can also be reached by using the crag-base path from below Makinodromo.

The first routes are on the main wall in a ravine behind a huge tilted block.

㉑ Comicos y modistas . . . 🕙 🖊 ☐ **6b+**
9m. A steep wall on interesting flowstone holds.

㉒ E.M. . . . . 🕙 🖐 ☐ **7a+**
9m. A juggy start leads to a crimpy and balancy finish.

㉓ Straw Donkey . . . . . 🕙 🖐 🖊 ☐ **7b**
10m. The blank wall with a series of flowstone pipes midway.

The overhanging front face of the huge tilted block contains a very hard but very short line

㉔ La tete de Mari . . . . 🖐 🖐 🖊 ☐ **8b**
7m. Steep bouldery moves up and left to finish.

Further to the right on the main cliff are two longer lines.

㉕ Not in the Bag . . . . 🕙 🖊 🖐 ☐ **(7c)**
22m. The left-leaning wall and arete is a very old line that may still not have been climbed.

㉖ In the Bag . . . . 🕙 🖐 🖊 ☐ **7c**
22m. The wall and shallow arete.

In front of from these routes, is a block with two lines of bolts and three climbs.

㉗ Hay un guarillo en la tapia . . . . ☐ **6a+**
7m. The left-hand line on the boulder.

㉘ Salto del gato I . . . . ☐ **6b**
7m. The central line.

㉙ Salto del gato II . . . . ☐ **6b+**
7m. A right-hand variation on *Salto del gato I* using the same bolts.

Routes start in deep ravine

Routes on the back of boulder

27 28
29
26
25

23
22
21
24

Los Tigres

The well-named Los Tigres wall is an orange, white and black streaked overhanging sheet of excellent rock. The climbing is sustained but not too strenuous. The wall faces the sun for much of the day and can be hot although it cools off in the evening when the sun moves off. Seepage can be a problem after prolonged rainfall.

Approach (see page 139) - The crag is usually approached from below. From the railway walk past a little hut 50m up the slope and continue on a path that gradually heads leftwards towards the cliff. It is best to continue up the path until just above the wall and then cut back down to the base of the routes. This avoids having to scramble over the large boulder field. It can also be reached by using the crag-base path from below Makinodromo.

❶ El segundo pegue ..   7c+
25m. The steep and slim right-to-left slanting corner and upper wall give a fine climb.

❷ La politica del piquillo
....   8a
27m. The big blank wall beneath the upper roof crack.

❸ Project ....   ?
27m. A line of bolts has been prepared but as yet do not reach the lower section of the wall.

❹ Guiris Go Home 7a
27m. Start up a short square-cut corner to gain the top of a block and then head on up the wall and cracks to finish on the right.

❺ El paso del Serengueti
....   8a
26m. The line starts just left of the initial crack of *La comunidad afro* and climbs parallel to it via a mid-height flake.

❻ La comunidad afro ....   7b+
26m. Start up a crack and gain a hole at 8m before progressing up the shallow rib above.

❼ Los autenticos tigres   8a+
27m. Start up *La comunidad afro* then move out on to the very blank wall to the right.

❽ Prisa mata ....   7c+
26m. The incredibly thin wall directly above the gearing up spot.

❾ Por puro vicio 7c
26m. An excellent wall climb with hard moves interspersed with good shakes. Start by a blob.

❿ El salto del tigre 8a
26m. A huge line up tufa and flowstone that sees plenty of attempts.

⓫ Life Will Never End 7c
26m. The right-hand line out of *El salto del tigre*.

⓬ New Line 8a
26m. The sustained wall and upper overhang.

⓭ The Speed Kings ......   7b+
26m. The fantastic pitch up huge leaning flowstone wall.

⓮ Los siete Larrys 7b
24m. Fine climbing on classic flowstone to a technical wall on blobs. *Photo opposite.*

⓯ Comando toxico 7b
24m. A disappointing line just right of *Los siete Larrys*.

To the right are a number of impressive corners and walls with some unfinished projects.

45 min · Lots of sun

Classic flowstone formations are just one facet of the beautiful wall climbs at sector Los Tigres. Mark Glaister samples the delights of *Los siete Larrys* (7b) - *opposite* . Photo: Alan Chapman (Glaister collection)

Mijas

Turon

Frontales

Escalera Arabe

Encantadas

The Gorge

Los Cvos

El Polvorin

Makinodromo

Desplomilandia

Andalajis

El Torcal

V. de Cauche

Archidona

Lola

1 Siempre fuimos punkies . . . . . [   ] 8a+
33m. On the far left of the crag. **7c** to first lower-off.

2 Trainspotting . . . . [   ] 8a
35m. A good and well-travelled route. To the first lower-off is **7b+**.

3 Samarkanda. . . [   ] 8b+
35m. A mind-blowing pitch that is very sustained.

4 El Oraculo . . . . [   ] 8b
35m. The sister line just to the right of *Samarkanda* that is **7c+** to its first lower-off.

5 El mono en el ojo del tigre. . [   ] 8b
35m. Another route that is **7c+** to the first lower-off.

6 Randi . . . . [   ] 8b
37m. The massive wall just left of the huge corner. To the first lower-off is **8a+**.

7 Que trabaje rita [   ] 8c+
40m. A monster line up the left-leaning corner. A variation goes left into *Randi* midway at **8c**. There are probably other new variations here as well.

8 Kuala lumpur . . [   ] 8c+
40m. The rounded arete, starting on the left.

9 Al-hakan . . . . [   ] 8c+
40m. The blank leaning wall to the left of *Lourdes* has a variation start to the left.

10 Lourdes. . . . . [Top 50] [   ] 8a
35m. Justifiably famous. An unrelenting pitch up the central line of tufas that sports a hard start and a pulse-enhancing finish. There are thankfully a few good shakeouts along the way.
Photo on page 39.

11 Conexion Lourdes . . [   ] 8a+
35m. A right-hand variation start to *Lourdes* following a steep set of tufas that meet up with the mother line midway.

12 Cous cous . . . . [Top 50] [   ] 8c
35m. An awesome pitch linking some large tufas and blobs on the lower wall and finishing up the protruding fin-like tufa in its second half.

13 Ceskoslovensko [   ] 8c
35m. Another hard line right of *Cous cous*.

14 Melanpina . . . . [   ] 8a+
33m. Impressive tufa stacks just left of the huge overhanging corner.

Lowering-off - The majority of the routes are much longer than 30m in length and very steep. Care is needed when lowering. It is possible to reach the ground on *Lourdes* with a 60m rope, but it is a close thing and there's nowhere to go if you find you are a few metres too short.

Lourdes

The massive tufa-draped over-hanging wall on the main section of Makinodromo is a breathtaking piece of rockscape and a beacon to climbers everywhere who are drawn to it to try one of the World's most famous sport routes - *Lourdes*. There are also a number of equally fine but even harder climbs that link clusters of tufa via fierce pocketed walls. The wall does see some shade late on in the day, or when the sun is high in the sky, but generally it is a hot venue.

Approach - See page 138 for a detailed description of the current approaches to Makinodromo.

The right-hand end of the huge overhanging wall runs into a very steep corner. The right wall of the huge overhanging corner gets shade until mid afternoon.

⑮ Smashing Pumpkins . . . 　 8a
30m. Start up the large pockets and tufa in the wall right of the huge overhanging corner and then veer left steeply above it.

⑯ Smashing Pumpkins Direct
. . . . 　 8a+
33m. Where the parent line veers left, continue steeply direct .

⑰ Atlas Shrieked . . . . 　 8a
35m. A stunning route following the well-positioned tufa on the arete to the right of the huge overhanging corner. Start up the first wall as for *Smashing Pumpkins*. **7c+** to the first lower-off.

⑱ Pepe el boludo. . . . 　 8a
35m. The wall overhang and short corner just right of the arete.

⑲ La dentellada. . . . . 　 8a+
35m. A thin wall and big overhang starting up *Pepe el boludo*.

⑳ Porrot . . . . 　 7c+
35m. The wall just right of the mid-height bulges. Sustained and pumpy but nothing desperate. *Photo on page 30.*

㉑ Mutenroy . . . . 　 8a
15m. The left-hand line of steepening tufa in the short alcove. Keep an eye out for a bee's nest.

㉒ Vete al infierno . . . . . . 　 7b
15m. The right-hand line of the alcove is tricky.

❶ Hakuna mata .... Top 50 7a+
32m. An excellent pitch. Start up the left-leaning ramp. Direct up the upper section is harder than the left-hand option.

❷ Al hauira 7b
32m. This line wanders around a bit low down and shares holds with *Hakuna mata*.

❸ Las loi laufen 7b
34m. A quality pitch that starts up the wall above the foot of the ramp and finishes through the upper bulges.

❹ Salida de emergencia .. 6c
17m. A popular but tricky little number. *Photo on page 9.*

❺ Estoy mortimer .... 7a+
18m. The left-hand line above the lower-off of *Salida de emergencia*. Low in the grade.

❻ Salida Extension 7b
24m. Right-hand line above the lower-off *Salida de emergencia* finishing through the highest roof.

❼ Mystic Rhythem ..... 6b+
26m. A good route taking on the right-hand side of the large central tufa to a lower-off.

❽ Rhythem Method 7b
34m. A right-hand variation to *Mystic Rhythem* is also worthwhile.

❾ La panda zampabollos. . 7b
34m. The direct start to *Rhythem Method*.

❿ La columna de gollum. . 7b
34m. The left side of the perfectly-formed tufa is taken mainly on the wall. Start via the downward-pointing cone-shaped tufa.

⓫ Columna Right .... (7c)
34m. Start up *Life is Sweet* and continue directly up the right side of the perfectly-formed tufa. Grade and name unconfirmed.

⓬ Life is Sweet .... Top 50 6c
32m. A brilliant and long pitch. Climb up to the downward-pointing cone-shaped tufa and pull up rightwards to gain the superb and pumpy upper wall. *Photo on page 136.*

Life is Sweet
A fabulous wall that complements the steeper and harder routes to its left. The wall is vertical and streaked with tufas, holes and pockets of all shapes and sizes. All the pitches are long and care is needed when lowering off - a 70m rope is a good idea.
Approach - Just around the corner from the Lourdes area is a narrow ramp that rises leftwards above the lower wall.

Lowering-off - Some of these pitches are longer than 30m in length. Take care when lowering off.

60 min | Lots of sun

See previous page

Mega Flash - 50m

Mijas
Tajon
Frontales
Escalera Arabe
Encantadas
The Gorge
Los Cotos
El Polveron
Makinodromo
Desplomilandia
Abdalajis
El Torcal
V. de Cauche
Archidona
Loja

⓭ Osama in the Sky . . . . . 🔆 📷 ▭ 7b+
32m. The steep grey wall on the right is tough all the way. Makes a good alternative start to *Life is Sweet* making it about **7a**.

⓮ Kolocotron . . . . 📷 🧗 ▭ 7a+
32m. A poor pitch up the wall just left of a vegetated corner.

⓯ Apache . . . . 🔆 📷 ▭ 6c+
32m. The wall and bulges.

⓰ Obama in the Whitehouse 🔆 📷 ▭ 6b+
32m. The wall to a bulging roof.

Sector Mega Flash

⓱ Anatema . . . . 🔆 🔧 ▭ 7b
10m. Short but very steep moves over the low roof.

⓲ Paracaidista cordobers . 🔆 🔧 ▭ 7c
10m. Similar climbing to its left-hand neighbour.

⓳ Heat Exchange . . . . 🔆 📷 ▭ 6c+
34m. Start right of a corner with a bush and climb the wild tufa and sustained wall above. *Photo on page 17.*

⓴ Canto pecato . . . . 🔆 🧗 ▭ 7b
22m. The gradually-steepening wall.

㉑ One bastiamba . . . . 🔆 📷 ▭ 7b
22m. Another dose of steep and sustained climbing up the bulging wall.

Mega Flash
A good but slightly deceptive sector that has a number of testing pitches that are far steeper than first appearances suggest.
Approach - Another 50m uphill from the Life is Sweet Wall is a steep section of horizontally banded rock, the first two short but steep lines are left of the main lines.

㉒ Post festum . . . . . . 🔆 🧗 🔧 ▭ 7b
22m. The wall just left of the corner chimney.

㉓ Mega Flash . . . . 🔆 🧗 ▭ 7a+
22m. Climb up through the overhang on some chipped holds.

㉔ Grimal el curtido . . . . 🔆 ▭ 7a
22m. A right-hand variation on *Mega Flash*.

㉕ Punk Street . . . . 🔆 📷 ▭ 7a
22m. Climb the wall into a prominent niche below the roof then out and over.

㉖ Putanaki . . . . 🔆 📷 🔧 ▭ 7b+
22m. Interesting climbing through a hole.

㉗ Reep . . . . 🔆 🔧 ▭ 7a+
23m. Steep and juggy but slippery at the final bulge.

A little further up the hillside is a very steep but low section of the cliff dubbed Mini Maki. It has four lines the grades from left to right being - **7c+,7a+,8a,7c**.

Mijas

Turon

Frontales

Escalera Árabe

Encantadas

The Gorge

Los Cotos

El Polvorín

Makinodromo

Desplomilandia

Abdalajís

El Torcal

V. de Cauche

Archidona

Loja

Desplomilandia

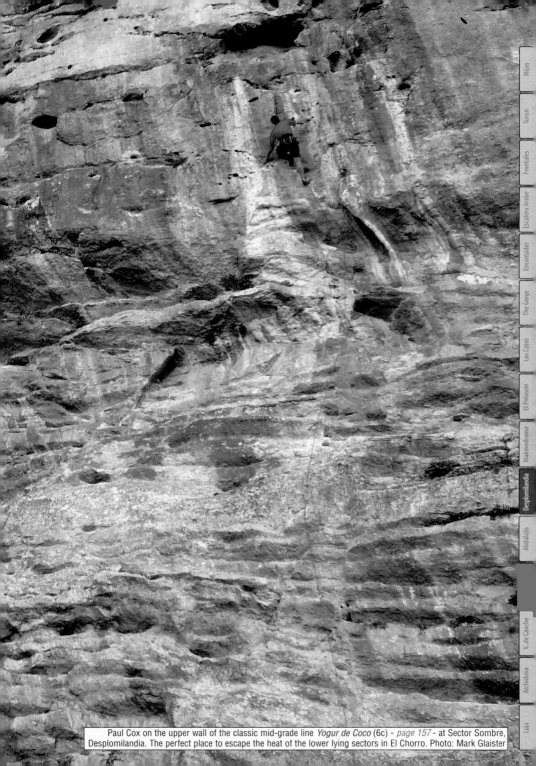

Mijas

Turón

Frontales

Escalera Árabe

Encantadas

The Gorge

Los Cotos

El Polvorín

Makinodromo

Desplomilandia

Abdalajís

V. de Cauche

Archidona

Loja

Paul Cox on the upper wall of the classic mid-grade line *Yogur de Coco* (6c) - *page 157* - at Sector Sombre, Desplomilandia. The perfect place to escape the heat of the lower lying sectors in El Chorro. Photo: Mark Glaister

Set in the hills way above the confines of El Chorro, and peering out over the picturesque turquoise lakes of Ardales, are the excellent crags that are collectively referred to as Desplomilandia. There is a good deal of climbing here for more experienced climbers but nothing really for those operating in the 'green spot' grades. For climbers looking for harder routes though, there is plenty on offer and all of it on immaculate rock, and in a shady setting. Desplomilandia has seen a lot of route development since the last Rockfax and this development continues along the base of the huge cliffs that stretch out to the east.

Approach

From El Chorro, cross the dam, turn right and follow a narrow winding road up hill out of the gorge for about 5km to a T-junction. Turn right and follow the road past lakes, a tunnel and a bar (*The Kiosko*). Cross a dam and pass through a village. A few kilometres further, after crossing another dam, follow signs for Antequera. The first crags appear on your right shortly after passing a couple of very large quarries. The first parking spot is at the base of a dirt track - park here for Sectors Buena Sombra and La Boda. For the other sectors, drive up the track to limited parking at a junction where another rough track on the right leads up to a col. This final section to the col is too rough to drive unless you are in a 4x4. Walk to the col from where paths lead to the various sectors. Sector Poza de la Mona is 3km further along the road towards Antequera see Sector notes on approach for parking and access details.

Conditions

Desplomilandia is higher and more exposed than the crags nearer to El Chorro and all of the sectors get a lot of shade. If things become too hot elsewhere then Desplomilandia is a haven of coolness. However even in winter the crags are usually in perfect condition although a coat might be needed when belaying and the sun is never far away from the base of the crag. There is some seepage after prolonged rainfall and climbing in the rain is possible at both sector Triangulo and Buena Sombra. There is no source of drinking water near by.

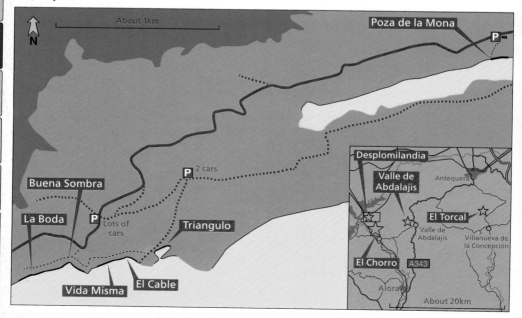

Mijas

Turón

Frontales

Escalera Arabe

Encantadas

The Gorge

Los Cotos

El Polvorín

Makinodromo

Desplomilandia

Abdalajís

El Torcal

V. de Cauche

Archidona

La conexión pelirroja (8a) - *page 152* - one of the many quality harder lines at El Triangulo, Desplomilandia. Photo: Mark Glaister

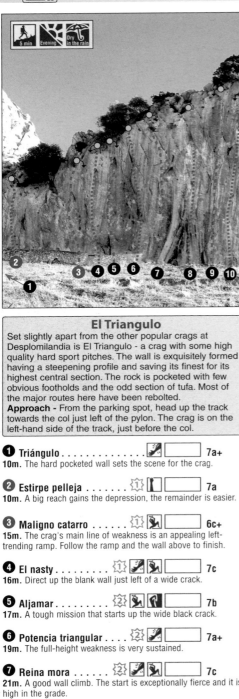

El Triangulo

Set slightly apart from the other popular crags at Desplomilandia is El Triangulo - a crag with some high quality hard sport pitches. The wall is exquisitely formed having a steepening profile and saving its finest for its highest central section. The rock is pocketed with few obvious footholds and the odd section of tufa. Most of the major routes here have been rebolted.

Approach - From the parking spot, head up the track towards the col just left of the pylon. The crag is on the left-hand side of the track, just before the col.

1 Triángulo . . . . 7a+
10m. The hard pocketed wall sets the scene for the crag.

2 Estirpe pelleja 7a
10m. A big reach gains the depression, the remainder is easier.

3 Maligno catarro . . . . . . 6c+
15m. The crag's main line of weakness is an appealing left-trending ramp. Follow the ramp and the wall above to finish.

4 El nasty 7c
16m. Direct up the blank wall just left of a wide crack.

5 Aljamar 7b
17m. A tough mission that starts up the wide black crack.

6 Potencia triangular . . . . 7a+
19m. The full-height weakness is very sustained.

7 Reina mora 7c
21m. A good wall climb. The start is exceptionally fierce and it is high in the grade.

8 Zeus kapotas . . . . ?
22m. A bolted but unfinished line that starts up the steep corner right of *Reina Mora*.

9 Mar de Ortigas . . . . Top 50 8a
25m. The classic of the crag gives incredibly sustained and immaculate climbing.

10 No toques a tu madre
. . . . 8a+
25m. A tight direct line with little chance of a rest.

11 Madre salvaje . . . . Top 50 7c
25m. The central line is a stunner that culminates in a punishing final crack.

12 Oasis de cristal . . . 7c
25m. The ramp and wall lead to a grossly overhanging finish.

13 La conexión pelirroja . . 8a
25m. An excellent line that features some hard wall climbing and a very sharp and steep upper crack. *Photos page 34 and 151.*

14 ¿Que tal mea tu padre? 7b
16m. Steep wall climbing to a hard last move.

15 Mas que money . . . . . . 7b+
16m. Sustained climbing finishing as for *¿Que tal mea tu padre?*

16 De copas 7b
16m. Move up through a black bulge to a high flake crack.

17 La copa 7b
16m. Make a steep start to a thin crack.

El Cable

A fine towering section of cliff with a handful of tremendous long pitches, on excellent rock and in a very beautiful setting. This sector does not receive any sunshine and is fairly exposed.

Approach - From the parking spot, head up the track towards the col just left of the pylon. The crag is on the right-hand side of the track, just before the col. The crag is also easily reached from the other lower Desplomilandia sectors by a good path that runs along the base of the cliff.

1 Maganto pro 6a
8m. Worthwhile climbing with a bit more on offer than appears at first glance.

2 Maganto 6a
9m. A good wall, bulge and rib.

3 Aprendiz de maganto . . 6a+
9m. Pull through the low overhang to the orange pocketed wall.

4 Good'un. . . . . 6a+
10m. The tricky little wall.

5 Puto cable 5
13m. The left-hand side of the depression.

6 Mareo repentino . . . 7a
17m. The thin wall passing an orange stain.

7 La flaca . . . . 6c+
28m. Start up a thin wall.

8 La decepción . . . . 7a+
30m. A good route starting by a small corner.

9 Uretrofilo 7a
30m. A very good pitch with some tricky moves.

10 Akira Top50 7b
30m. The shallow groove gives an excellent and difficult climb.

11 Donde estan mis amigos 7b+
32m. A very blank orange wall past two holes

12 Oleanna . . . . . . 7b+
32m. The blank and crimpy wall.

13 Project . . . .
32m. The wall right of *Oleanna*.

14 Mamabi. 7b
1) 6b, 12m. The wall and left-curving line to a ledge.
2) 7b, 20m. The tufa and steep ground above.

Lowering-off - Some of these pitches are longer than 30m in length. Take care when lowering off.

Not much sun
5 min

Mijas
Turon
Frontales
Escalera Arabe
Encantadas
The Gorge
Los Cotos
El Polvorin
Makinodromo
Desplomilandia
Abdalajis
El Torcal
V. de Cauche
Archidona
Loja

Aro de santo

The first three routes are on the far left section of crag that is actually the right-hand side of the El Cable Sector.

1 El angel flamenco 7a
26m. A long route that starts right of the arete. Old bolts.

2 Aro de santo .... 6c+
26m. A deceptively difficult start involving some lock-offs on good slots. The name of the route is painted on the rock.

3 Maritobi .... 6a+
16m. A smashing little pitch with some intriguing leftward moves and a steep ending.

4 Ostras pedrin 5
18m. A good easier route.

5 Al loro con el Xato . 6c+
18m. Fine technical wall work.

6 Manzanilla Madness ... 7a
24m. Tricky climbing over the bottom bulge, which is best tackled from the right. Above this, things are a little reachy.

7 Cheyenne .... 7a+
20m. Nice wall climbing, with a pressing finish to gain the still awkward slab.

Al Andalu

⑧ Maquina pestosa .. 7b+
18m. More good sustained climbing which starts up the steep tufa before a bouldery move gains easier ground.

⑨ Ankana wanamio .. 8a+
18m. The left-hand line of bolts leading out from *Al andalú* has a surprisingly decent amount of independent climbing.

⑩ Al andalú 6c
18m. A really good line that is a touch on the worn side, but still one of the best here.

⑪ Sandokan 7c
28m. Impressive climbing up the left-hand side of the arete.

⑫ Si te gustael pique, pique 6b
22m. A lovely pitch with a surprising amount of climbing.

⑬ Captain sardina 6c
30m. An excellent companion to *Si te gustael pique, pique* climbing the slim ramp and headwall.

⑭ Espurga perros 6c
23m. Good climbing up the orange left wall of the corner.

La Vida Misma

A long shady escarpment of excellent and well-featured rock. The pleasing grade spread makes this a popular spot. The wall does not receive much sun in the wintertime but is rarely too cold and suffers little from seepage.
Approach - From the parking spot, walk up the track towards the col and pylon. Just before the col, a path leads off to the right to Sector El Cable and just around its right arete is the start of La Vida Misma.

⑮ Calidad alemana 6b
30m. The popular orange corner is nicely sustained.

⑯ El emigrante . . . . 7a+
25m. The blunt right arete of the corner of *Calidad alemana.*

⑰ El chupacabras . . . . 7a+
24m. A dramatic pitch which makes up for its lack of length with some fine moves. Go easy with the large fragile flake, in fact give it a miss altogether!

⑱ Zulu Master . . . . 7a+
24m. The wall on the far right.

⑲ Chica . . . . 5+
20m. A line down and right of *Zulu Master.* Not on topo.

7 min · Evening

Espurga perros

12 13 14 15 16 17 18 19

Mijas · Turon · Frontales · Escalera Arabe · Encantadas · The Gorge · Los Cotos · El Polvorin · Makinodromo · Desplomilandia · Abdalajis · El Torcal · V. de Cauche · Archidona · Loja

1 Dolomiti . . . . ⟨1⟩ 🔌 [ ] **7a+**
13m. Start from the top of the iron rungs on the left.

2 Fran sin natra. . . . . ⟨2⟩ 🔌 [ ] **7b**
13m. The first line on the wall is always well chalked. Intense.

3 Perseverancia . . . . ⟨2⟩ [ ] **8a**
32m. The buging wall above *Fran sin natra*.

4 Paquistani . . . . ⟨3⟩ 🔌 [ ] **8a**
32m. Head left from first lower-off on *Liron careto*.

5 Liron careto . . . . ⟨3⟩ 🔌 [ ] **7c**
32m. A superb climb. The steep top section is **7c** and the lower wall to a lower-off is a popular **7a** in its own right.

6 Escombros . . . . ⟨1⟩ 🔌 [ ] **5+**
14m. The short left-hand line is good.

7 Autan . . . . ⟨1⟩ 🔌 [ ] **5+**
14m. Similar to *Escombros* but perhaps a little easier.

8 Champion Leo . . . . 💪 🔌 [ ] **8b?**
32m. A long standing project.

9 Los zauden . . . . . . ⟨2⟩ 🔌 🪝 [ ] **8a**
34m. A good **7a** first section via a steep tufa.

10 Derribamitos . . . . ⟨2⟩ 🪝 [ ] **8a**
40m. Very steep in its upper half.

11 A ella le gusta la gasolina
. . . . ⟨3⟩ 🔌 🪝 [ ] **8a**
40m. The right-hand line out of *Derribamitos*.

12 La golosa . . . . ⟨3⟩ 🔌 🪝 [ ] **7c+**
40m. Start just to the left of the iron rungs and climb direct.

13 El montepio de cretinos . . . . . . [ ] **8a**
40m. A monster pitch passing mid-height tree on the right.

14 Escalador parasito . . . . [ ] **?**
22m. A project starting from the top of rungs.

15 Las gallas . . . . [ ] **7b+**
22m. The right-hand line from the top of the rungs.

16 El comite de sabios . . . . [ ] **8a**
40m. Start just right of the base of the rungs.

Not much sun · 3 min · Dry in the rain

Line of rungs

Line of rungs

Sector Buena Sombra

A fine section of cliff that has been fully developed since the last Rockfax guide. The bulging wave-like rock is covered with pockets, jugs and tufas giving routes of length and variety. The left-hand section has mainly long hard and steep pitches and the right-hand side is less steep and has many full-height mid-grade routes. The lines are fairly close together and although the names of some routes are painted on the rock, it can still be a little confusing so spend some time picking out your precise line before you set off. The crag offers dry climbing during wet spells.
Approach - From the parking, walk back along the road and take a good path on the left that leads quickly to the base of the cliff.

Lowering-off - Some of these pitches are longer than 30m in length. Take care when lowering off.

Mijas · Turon · Frontales · Escalera Arabe · Encantadas · The Gorge · Los Cotos · El Polvorin · Makinodromo · Desplomilandia · Abdalajis · El Torcal · V. de Cauche · Archidona · Loja

17 Judas 7b
38m. Start up the grey groove to the right of the iron rungs and tackle the steep bulge via a tufa.

18 El ruin de Roma 7c
37m. The wall and bulges above. Low in the grade.

19 Viejos y puretas 7a
30m. A popular pitch with a hard bulge. *Photo on page 36.*

20 Cosas caseras . . . . 7a+
32m. Similar to *Viejos y Puretas* but more sustained and better.

21 Tarde pero perfecto . . . . 6c+
26m. Share the last bolt with *Yogur de Coco*.

22 Yogur de Coco 6c
26m. Pass to the left of the midway tufa. *Photo on page 148.*

23 Comando escandilla . . . 6c+
30m. The right-hand side of the tufa requires a bit of a reach.

24 Hilando fino 7b
30m. The very thin wall via some drilled pockets.

25 Buena sombre . . . . 6b+
30m. A fine line past some shallow tufas at mid-height.

26 Alobeitor . . . . 6a+
30m. Marvellous wall climbing on pockets.

27 Sin mantenimiento 6a
30m. A smart climb with lots of hidden holds.

28 Provinciano marrano . . . 6c
30m. Move up a short wall and then climb the upper wall on small holds to a steep juggy finish.

29 Debora cuerpos . . . 6b
30m. Climb the initial short blank wall via a hidden pocket and high edge. The upper wall is superb.

30 Menasatrua . . . . 6a+
22m. Steep pocket-pulling up a blank wall. Start up a slanting ramp from the right.

31 Efecto secundario . . . . . 6b+
22m. The thin wall with a delicate sequence to get started.

32 Vaya pieza 6b
22m. A lovely pitch with a good thin and fingery climbing.

33 El Arco 6b
30m. An old trad line following the left-trending overhang.

34 Las cosillas . . . . 6c+
20m. A hard start up the edge of the overhang.

35 Las cosas de mike 6b
20m. The left-hand bolts of two very close lines.

36 La pyme 6b
20m. The right-hand line is the last on the wall.

Not much sun

3 min

Mijas · Túron · Frontales · Escalera Árabe · Encantadas · The Gorge · Los Cotos · El Polvorín · Makinodromo · Desplomilandia · Abdalajís · El Torcal · V. de Caudie · Archidona · Loja

La Boda

A very pleasant section of crag that has lots of good mid-grade pitches and a few harder ones. The rock is not polished and has some sharp holds. At busy times this area of cliff is often much quieter than the rest.

Approach - From the parking at the bottom of the dirt track, walk back along the road and take a path on the left that leads to the base of Sector Buena Sombra. Head up rightwards on a steep path at the base of the cliff to the sectors where the path levels off.

1 Sarathoga . . . . 6c+
23m. The thin grey wall on the left-hand side of the sector is much tougher than first appearances would suggest.

2 Perisca 6b
23m. A deceptively tricky line with some thought provoking moves.

3 Liposuccion 7b
13m. Finger pockets up the left arete.

4 Madera de higuera . . . . 7a+
13m. The pocketed wall to the right of the arete is pretty good.

5 Puta parietaria . . . . 7a+
16m. Steep climbing up the grey-streaked wall via two pockets.

6 El testigo . . . . 7a+
16m. The wall past a small triangular niche.

7 Project . . . . ?
28m. Up a hanging grey rib.

8 Connecting People . 7b+
26m. A hard pocketed red wall.

9 Bichaca 7c
24m. The bulging wall has some good pockets that are connected by some difficult thin wall moves with more hard climbing near the top.

10 Bulging Orange . . . . . . 8a+
20m. The very steep wall to the right of *Bichaca*.

11 Project . . . . ?
16m. A steep bolted line at the upper end of the ramp right of *Bulging Orange*.

Perisca

Bichaca

Mijas · Turón · Frontales · Escalera Árabe · Encantadas · The Gorge · Los Cotos · El Polvorín · Makinodromo · Desplomilandia · Abdalajís · El Torcal · V. de Cauche · Archidona · Loja

12 La fea . . . . 5+
30m. The left-hand rib of the sector starting up the corner.

13 Yolinda . . . . 6b+
15m. A short pitch up the blank wall.

14 El novio . . . . 6c+
30m. Super sustained wall climbing that has its hardest climbing at the start.

15 Beshumiau . . . . 7a+
30m. An eliminate line direct up the brown wall.

16 La novia 7a
30m. One of the best on this sector with varied and interesting climbing. A bit run out in places.

17 La suegra 6c
27m. Start up a steep pocketed wall above a ledge at 2m.

18 Diente de elefante 6b
27m. Start up the rib and pocketed crack just right of the ledge at 2m.

19 El anillo perdido . . . . . . 6a+
27m. Climb direct up to, and past, a high diamond-shaped hole.

20 La marcha atras 6c
26m. Start between bushes and climb the orange streak right of the diamond-shaped hole.

El anillo perdido

12 13 14 15 16 17 18 19 20

Mijas · Turon · Frontales · Escalera Arabe · Encantadas · The Gorge · Los Cotos · El Polvorin · Makinodromo · Desplomilandia · Abdalajis · El Torcal · V. de Cauche · Archidona · Loja

Poza de la Mona

Located away from the bulk of the crags at Desplomilandia, the long low walls of Poza de la Mona offer two distinctly different climbing areas. The left end of the crag gives some interesting lines, mainly following wide cracks and vertical walls that, although not particularly impressive, are on good rock and in the shade for a large part of the day. The right-hand side of the crag is much larger and steeper and has some fine routes on a compact and steep face.

Approach - From the main parking area below Desplomilandia, continue along the main road for a further 3km until the crag comes into view on the right. Park next to an abandoned farm below the crag and take a good path up to the crag from where all the climbs are easily reached.

Access - Previously this approach was not used due to problems with the now-departed farmer. Should the farm become active again, or the property redeveloped, the old approach via a path next to a small valley that starts at a bend well before the farm should be used.

① **Entre higos** **6a**
10m. The crozzly crack behind a tree at the left-hand end of the crag.

② **Laguna betiko** **6b**
20m. Start up a right-trending ramp and climb direct up the left-hand bolt line.

③ **Buen amigo** **6a**
20m. Start up the ramp of *Laguna betiko* and continue up the right-hand bolt line.

④ **Puerco Arana** . . . . **5+**
26m. A long wall pitch to a lower-off at a roof.

⑤ **Parecia tonta** **6a**
11m. The pleasant wall left of a wide crack/runnel.

⑥ **Esa bavaresa** **6b**
11m. The wide crack/runnel.

⑦ **Flora** **6a**
11m. Take the wall and pockets left of a keyhole feature at 4m.

⑧ **Fauna** . . . . **6a+**
12m. Ascend a runnel, passing a small tree.

⑨ **Cerebro de broca** **6a**
12m. The steep pocketed wall and cracks.

⑩ **Kira la bulti** **6a**
15m. The wide cracks.

⑪ **Siempre Juli** . . . . **6a+**
15m. A rounded wide crack to eventually join up with the upper section of *Kira la bulti*.

⑫ **Ras cubano** **6a**
17m. The bolted thin left-hand crack up a tall white wall.

⑬ **Las gordas no dan resaca** **6b+**
17m. The right-hand bolted crack up the white wall.

The crag navigation tabs on right side: Mijas, Turon, Frontales, Escalera Arabe, Encantadas, The Gorge, Los Cotos, El Polvorin, Makinodromo, Desplomilandia, Abdalajis, El Torcal, V. de Cauche, Archidona, Loja

⑭ Colourful crack . . . . 6b?
13m. The crack on the far left side of the wall.

⑮ Deate de rollo . . . . 🔧 6b+
15m. A difficult wall pitch passing a hole at 4m.

⑯ Subete a la higuera . . . . 🔧🖐 6a+
15m. A series of disjointed tufas just left of a tree at the base of the crag.

⑰ Poda higuera . . . . 🔧🖐 6b
16m. The cracks and pockets just right of the tree are more of an undertaking than they appear at first glance.

⑱ Abrasiva . . . . 🔧🔧 6c
16m. The wall via a pocket and thin cracks to finish as for *Poda higuera*. The start is bouldery.

⑲ Malva loca 7a
16m. A long and rounded crack.

⑳ Feltan negro . . . . 🔧🔧 7b
17m. The excellent but difficult thin crack system up the orange wall right of *Malva loca*.

㉑ Arquitectura moderna . . 🔧🔧 7a+
18m. The wall just to the left of *Bee Bee* requires a very fingery pull midway.

㉒ Bee Bee . . . . 🔧🔧 6c+
22m. The classic of the crag. Follow the left-trending pocketed groove to a rest and finish up the tufas on the right. Well worn but the holds are nearly all massive. *Photo on page 41.*

㉓ Pina disfruta . . . . . 🔧🔧🔧 7b+
21m. The short tufa and pocketed brown crozzly streak just right of *Bee Bee*.

㉔ Vas de guais . . . . . 🔧🔧🔧 7c
21m. The hard wall and thin cracks behind a tree at the base of the crag.

㉕ Leaning meany . . . . 7c?
22m. The bulges to twinned thin cracks.

㉖ Silicona Beach . . . . 🔧🔧🔧 7b+
23m. Difficult climbing up an orange streak.

㉗ Excrementos . . . . 🔧 7a+
25m. The enticing left-leaning orange corner starting from a raised ledge.

㉘ Hirakundia . . . . 🔧🔧 7c
26m. Traces the stunning line of left-trending thin cracks right of the corner of *Excrementos*.

㉙ Prosineski . . . . 🔧🔧🔧 7c+
32m. An unbalanced line starting up tufa drapes next to a tree at the right end of the raised ledge. Finish up the steep walls above to the top.

㉚ Lola . . . . 🔧 7a+?
14m. A steep line that joins up with the final move of *Alacran*.

㉛ Alacran . . . . 🔧🔧 7b+
14m. The overhanging wall on pockets to a chain lower-off.

㉜ Amor al arte . . . . 🔧🔧 7b
15m. A short and very steep bulging wall.

㉝ Calorin 5
17m. A poor pitch up the easy-angled right-hand rib of the crag.

㉞ Ambiente selecto . . . . 6b+
14m. A steep pitch that starts from a ledge above *Amor al arte*.

Valle
de Abdalajis

Mijas

Turón

Frontales

Escalera Arabe

Encantadas

The Gorge

Los Cotos

El Polvorin

Makinodromo

Desplomlandia

Abdalajis

El Torcal

V. de Cauche

Archidona

Loja

The impressive fractured wall of Sector Fisuras at Valle de Abdalajis provides some very long crack climbs such as *Fisuras armoniosas* (6a+) - *page 166*. Climber: Dave Henderson. Photo: Mark Glaister

Mijas

Turon

Frontales

Escalera Arabe

Encantadas

The Gorge

Los Cotos

El Polvorin

Makinodromo

Desplomilandia

Abdalajis

El Torcal

V. de Cauche

Archidona

Loja

At the far end of the southern face of the mountain range that holds the bulk of El Chorro's climbing lie the charming tiered walls and slabs of Valle de Abdalajis. The climbing is on excellent limestone and of a friendly nature with the added bonus of expansive views and dawn to dusk sunshine. There are plenty of well-bolted lines in the grades from 4 to 6a+ making it a good spot for teams with mixed abilities or those just finding their feet. The areas described are only minutes from the car parking area and the various sectors are well marked with signs at the base of the cliff.

This is a lovely area and has vast potential for lots of new routes at moderate grades both short and multi-pitch. Development of the whole area is continuing apace so expect new routes here.

Approach

From the railway station at El Chorro, take the road signed to Valle de Abdalajis which goes up the hill and passes under Las Encantadas. The road winds its way over the range, turning left at the only major road junction, and then slowly drops until the outskirts of Valle de Abdalajis come into view. The crags are easily seen up on the left. Take the road into the village and follow it as it contours above the main centre of the village down to the right. After a few hundred metres a small sign for El Chorro will be seen on the left. Turn sharp left here (this is the first turning on the left that actually leads anywhere and is just before a no entry sign).

The narrow road soon turns into a rough track and leads out of the built-up area and towards the crags. After 0.7km a number of small gravel tracks lead off to the right before a small farm building on the right is reached, take one of the tracks depending on which end of the crag you want to park at. From the parking spots a number of paths lead quickly up to the base of the crag. The sectors are easily identified by large signs at their respective bases and a good series of small paths allow quick and easy access between the various sectors.

Conditions

The crags face south and receive sun all day. There is absolutely no shade at their base making this an extremely hot place to climb. Take plenty of water, sun block and a hat. In windy or wet weather it is best to climb elsewhere since the open slabs are exposed to the elements.

Teams enjoying the line up of well bolted easier routes on Sector Central at Valle de Abdalajis - *page 168*. Photo: Mark Glaister

Sector Diagonal

Sector Central

Sector Fisuras

Sector Escalon

Track from Valle de Abdalajis

Mijas
Turon
Frontales
Escalera Arabe
Encantadas
The Gorge
Los Cotos
El Polvorin
Makinodromo
Desplomilandia
Abdalajis
El Torcal
V. de Cauche
Archidona
Loja

3 min | Lots of sun

Lowering-off - Some of these pitches are longer than 30m in length. Take care when lowering off.

Sector Diagonal

Sector Fisuras

The large, mosaic-cracked wall of Sector Fisuras is the most impressive area of rock developed so far along the front range of the crags at Valle de Abdalajis. The best lines are all long and require care when lowering off. On some of the climbs this will require an abseil, or a two stage lower-off, unless a 70m rope is used.

Approach - From the various parking spots good paths lead easily to the left end of the developed area where a large purpose-built sign indicates the sector.

There are a number of short bolted lines on the walls to the left of those shown on the topo.

① Menos mal? . . . . **4+**
10m. Useful more as a locater than as a route. This line is the corner crack and wall set a couple of metres back from the main face at the left-hand side of the main wall.

② Esto desploma? **5**
12m. Climb to the same lower-off as *Menos mal?*

③ Elecciones 99 . . . . **6c**
13m. An unfinished line up the left edge of the wall.

④ La bavaresa . . . . **5+**
16m. The left-trending thin crack system.

⑤ Fisura devoradora . . . . . **4+**
30m. The bolted off-width crack.

⑥ Artelo martelo **5**
30m. The all-consuming, never-ending, left-leading crack can be a little green early in the season.

⑦ Dedos sangrientos **5**
34m. Take the *Artelo martelo* to the upper right diagonal crack and follow this to the top. The name means 'Bloody Fingers' - beware!

⑧ Cantolandia **6a**
35m. Fine climbing that reaches and then follows the cracks up the wall right of *Artelo martelo*.

⑨ Fisuras armoniosas. **6a+**
35m. An harmonious climb that combines a technical lower section with some cracking manoeuvres high up. The pitch can be split at a lower-off and stance at 9m. *Photo on page 162.*

⑩ Ozu! Esto como es?. **6b**
35m. A huge pitch that tackles the blanker section of the wall towards its right-hand side. The pitch can be split at a lower-off and stance at 9m (the same one as on *Fisuras armoniosas*).

⑪ Poderio vertical **5**
9m. The short crack, just left of the tree, to a lower-off.

⑫ Despo Wall **6c**
12m. The short hard wall.

Sector Diagonal

Sector Diagonal is basically the right-hand continuation of the Sector Fisuras wall but is less featured. It is distinguished easily by two parallel diagonal cracks running leftwards up the right-hand side of the wall.

Approach - From the various parking spots good paths lead easily to the left end of the developed area where a large purpose built sign indicates the sector.

13 El olvillo del osilllo .... 5+
18m. The entertaining runnel to a lower-off at its top.

14 Un pobre infeliz ... 4+
18m. The lovely open wall and breaks.

15 Right Turn 6a
35m. Move out right from midway up *Un pobre infeliz*. Descend in two stages, via the lower-off on the other routes, unless you have a 70m rope.

16 Horno dulferiensis 6a
35m. The bolted left-hand diagonal to a mid-height lower-off.

17 El hueso 6a
1) 6a, 20m. The right-hand crack is not bolted and requires a full rack. The stance at a ledge and tree is bolted.
2) 5+, 15m. The corner crack above gains a bolted abseil point.

Mijas
Túron
Frontales
Escalera Arabe
Encantadas
The Gorge
Los Cotos
El Polvorín
Makinodromo
Desplomilandia
Abdalajis
El Torcal
V. de Cauche

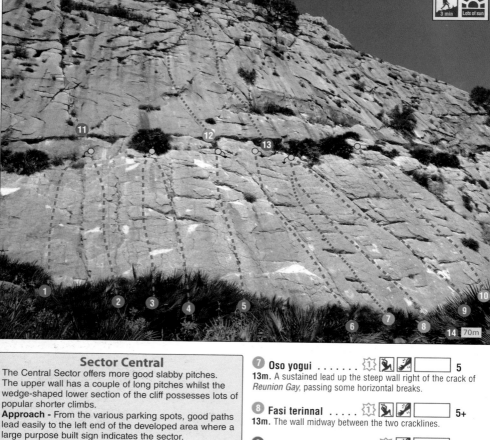

Sector Central

The Central Sector offers more good slabby pitches. The upper wall has a couple of long pitches whilst the wedge-shaped lower section of the cliff possesses lots of popular shorter climbs.

Approach - From the various parking spots, good paths lead easily to the left end of the developed area where a large purpose built sign indicates the sector.

❶ Supertrepaero . . . . 3+
9m. The wall to the left of a short crack.

❷ Terricola . . . . 3+
10m. The slim wall between cracks.

❸ Los currantes 4
11m. Another clean wall.

❹ Albert extrem 4
11m. The indefinate crack to widening after mid-height.

❺ Er Suzuki . . . . 4+
12m. A good pitch up the wall to the left of a plant at two-thirds height.

❻ Reunion Gay 4
13m. The full-height thin crack is another short but very worthwhile climb.

❼ Oso yogui 5
13m. A sustained lead up the steep wall right of the crack of *Reunion Gay*, passing some horizontal breaks.

❽ Fasi terinnal . . . . . 5+
13m. The wall midway between the two cracklines.

❾ BuBu 4
13m. Climb the prominent left-leaning crackline to a bush and lower-off.

❿ Bano de tierra 5
13m. The last of the pitches on the lower section of the crag.

⓫ La Diagonal . . . . 6b+
60m. The gradually-widening crackline is a huge trad pitch that is unfortunately heavily vegetated at the present time.

⓬ A pleno sol 6a
26m. A well-positioned, long and technical pitch.

⓭ Los Profesionales . . 6c
26m. The sustained wall starting from the right. Finish at the same lower-off as *A pleno sol*.

⓮ Mascha and Niko . . . . 6b+
25m. A lone pitch about 70m right of the other routes.

Mijas | Túron | Frontales | Escalera Arabe | Encantadas | The Gorge | Los Cotos | El Polvorin | Makinodromo | Descimlandia | Abdalajis | El Torcal | V. de Cascada | Ardo

15 Blokes Like Us 5
17m. The rib to a terrace and then the wall to a lower-off right of a large flake.

16 Chicharreta . . . . 4+
8m. The wall right of a very short crack has three bolts.

17 La corta 5
8m. The very slim corner.

18 Barre que barre 5
9m. A thin crack leads to moves right to finish at a lower-off.

19 El valle 5
10m. Cracks leading left to the top.

20 Musgogenesis 6a
12m. Thin face climbing to easier ground above.

21 Fisurón . . . . 4+
12m. The wide central crack.

22 Esquerra 5
13m. Climb the face to a thin crackline in the upper wall.

23 Adherencia extrema . . . 4+
13m. The finger-crack to a narrow wall.

Sector Escalon

Another slabby section of wall which is very popular and has lots of short pitches that are on average a bit tougher than those on Sector Central.

Approach - From the various parking spots, a number of paths head rightwards to the wall that is sited just above and to the left of a small quarry. The quarry is a good place to park if climbing at this end of the crag. Paths lead along the base of the crag to the other sectors described.

24 La mejó 5
13m. A long face climb to the left of the tree.

25 Lefty . . . . 5+
17m. The face just to the right of the tree.

26 November Rain 5
17m. The right-most line on this section.

60m further to the right are two final lines.

27 Wish You Were Here, Spocky! . 5
17m. The left-hand of the two routes.

28 Welcome to the Jungle 5
1) 4, 17 m. Trend rightwards to the stance.
2) 5, 23m. A crack system to the top. Abseil off - 35m!

El Torcal

Mijas
Turon
Frontales
Escalera Arabe
Encantadas
The Gorge
Los Cotos
El Polvorin
Makinodromo
Desplomilandia
Abdalajis
El Torcal
V' de Cauche
Archidona
Loja

Crystal clear conditions on the excellent roadside warm-up *Asfalto* (6a) - *page 174* - at Sector La Carretera, El Torcal. Photo: Paul Cox (Glaister collection).

Mijas

Turón

Frontales

Escalera Arabe

Encantadas

The Gorge

Los Cotos

El Polvorín

Makinodromo

Desplomilandia

Abdalajís

El Torcal

V. de Gauche

Archidona

Loja

The small National Park of El Torcal sits at an elevation of 1300m and forms the summit and slopes of a large limestone peak, around 10km to the south of the town of Antequera. The summit area of the peak is a broad plateau that has been heavily eroded to form some fantastic limestone 'karst' scenery - a geological curiosity. The karst formations present an amazing climbers' playground, set amidst a myriad of spectacular pinnacles and spires. The shallow grassy valleys and hollows between the pinnacles make lovely picnic and sunbathing spots making El Torcal a very pleasant place to visit. A good deal of the plateau has been climbed on over the years but a ban on some of the areas adjacent to the Visitor Centre has been imposed, however, the areas described in this chapter are all without restrictions and are well worth seeking out. Much of the climbing is highly technical and, although often less than 15m in height, the pitches are sustained and in magnificent surroundings.

Approach

From El Chorro, take the winding paved road up the hill past Las Encantadas, to the town of Valle de Abdalajis. Go through the town and turn left onto the main Antequera road. Continue for 20km towards Antequera. This main road can also be reached by driving around to the lakes above The Gorge and picking up the road to the north of the El Chorro massif. Just before Antequera is reached, turn right (signed 'El Torcal de Antequera') and follow the road up and around the side of the mountain, for about 10km, to the park entrance. Drive into the park and follow the road up the hill to reach the visitor centre at its end. This drive takes about 1 hour from El Chorro.

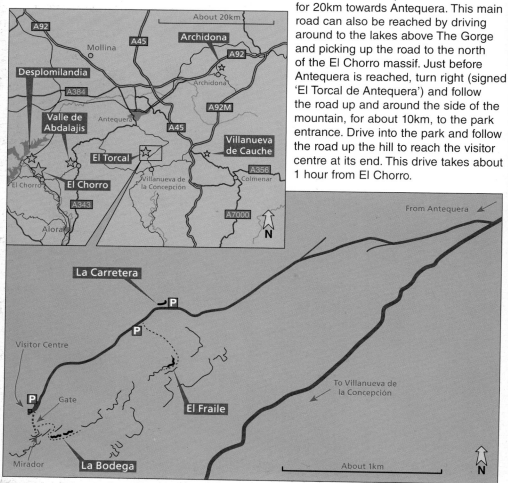

Mijas

Túron

Frontales

Escalera Arabe

Encantadas

The Gorge

Los Cotos

El Polvorín

Makinodromo

Desplomilandia

Abdalajís

El Torcal

V. de Cautche

Archidona

Loja

Conditions

The altitude can make it chilly at times and during the winter it is probably worth avoiding if it is at all windy or cloudy. However, on a still winter's day, once the sun has warmed the place up, it can take on a magical atmosphere. Much of the climbing faces south but there are a few north facing routes for those here in the hotter months. The altitude makes El Torcal worth considering in order to escape the extreme heat.

Debbie Binns high above the village of Villanueva de la Concepción on *Cruzcampo* (6a+) - *page 177* - on the stunningly located Sector La Bodega at El Torcal. Photo: Chris Sims

Sector La Carretera

A compact wall of excellent rock that provides some intense pitches which are easily found but not as easily ticked! Very convienient and worth stopping off at if only for the excellent *Asfalto*.

Approach - The first roadside wall on the right as the road levels after reaching the plateau from the park entrance.

❶ Domingacios Crack 7a
11m. The crack on the far left to the tree.

❷ Ero ergo sur 7a
21m. The wall left of the wide (unclimbed) crack. The start is vegetated at present.

❸ Mercedes 26 años . 7b
21m. A hard climb up the central wall via a small overlap.

❹ Asfalto . . . . Top 50 6a
22m. Fine moves up the open groove. *Photo on page 170.*

❺ La fuerza del destino 7b+
21m. A vicious bouldery start gains the lovely upper wall.

Sector El Fraile

❻ Exitos encadenados 6c+
18m. The far left-hand wall started from a high ledge.

❼ Sacrifice 7b
22m. Start up *Maldonado cabron* and branch left up wall.

❽ Maldonado cabron 6b
22m. The left-hand crack line to the top.

❾ Los golfos del golfo . . . 6b
14m. A good but short crack to a mid-height lower-off.

❿ Blank Wall 8a
22m. The desperate blank wall.

⓫ Mala reputacion . . . . . . 6c+
22m. The line of shallow cracks.

⓬ A vista de pájaro 7a
22m. The blank wall direct. Name painted at base.

Sector El Fraile

A beautifully situated crag with a reasonable spread of grades but nothing particularly easy. The walls are much bigger than might be imagined and the view is stunning.

Approach - It is not far from the road but is tricky to locate. From the parking area 150m beyond sector La Carretera, walk back down the road for 70m and pick up a faint path on the right that leads through some thorny bushes and under a power-line. Head for the col on the near horizon. The crag is just over the col on the right.

Choralasmirlas Froe

13 Hotel California 🔲🔲🔲🔲 **7a+**
22m. The wall past the left side of a tiny overhang. Name at base.

14 Turboniajas ...... 🔲🔲🔲 **7a**
22m. The wall past the centre of a tiny overhang.

15 Villanueva City....... 🔲🔲 **6b**
22m. Debolted at the present time. Name at base.

16 El trepaollas ..... 🔲🔲🔲 **6a+**
22m. A line of thin cracks on the right side of the wall.

17 La grieta de Julieta.... 🔲🔲 **5**
18m. Good climbing up the crack and flakeline.

18 Paraiso de los cazos romos
. . . . 🔲🔲🔲 **7a**
17m. The arete to the right of the corner crack.

19 Pillar. . . . . 🔲🔲 **6c+**
15m. The pillar to the right of a corner.

20 La calentona .... 🔲🔲 **7a**
15m. The crack past a bush.

21 Calentamientos ...... 🔲🔲 **6c+**
15m. The wall past a bush.

22 Choralasmirlas froe ... 🔲🔲 **6a**
16m. A groove and crack up the left side of rounded pillar.

23 Arete. . . . . 🔲 **(7b+)**
16m. Grade unknown.

24 Dos Ryobis y un destino 🔲🔲 **7b+**
21m. Power through the first bulge to the easier wall above.

25 La union hace la fiesta . 🔲🔲 **7a**
21m. A line just left of corner.

26 Té en el Sahara . . . 🔲🔲 **8a+**
30m. Start up the bulging crack before heading up the arete.

27 Hierba Luisa . . 🔲🔲🔲🔲 **8b+**
30m. Start up the steep groove right of the crack.

28 Menta poleo. . . 🔲🔲🔲🔲 **8c**
30m. A huge bulging wall to the left of the mid-height overhang.

29 Un-named .... 🔲🔲🔲🔲 **8a**
30m. Direct via the mid-height overhang.

30 Cowboy . . . . 🔲🔲 **7b**
30m. The exposed rampline in the headwall. Older bolts

Hierba Luisa

Martini Bianco

Nicey

10 min Lots of sun Windy

1 2 3

50m gap

4 5 6 7

8 9 10 11

Sector La Bodega

A good little area with lots of short routes on great rock and with a stunning view down to the coast.

Approach (see map on page 172) - Although only a stone's throw from the Mirador, this sector is pretty tricky to find, so go slowly! Park at the visitor centre and take the path to the Mirador. Looking straight ahead, a short pinnacle can be seen about 100m away on the edge of the escarpment. This is where routes 1, 2 and 3 are located. Back track a few metres to a gate and take a path behind it which is vague for the first 5m. Follow the rocky boot-worn path for 130m until it drops down into a shallow gully. At this point loop back hard right under the large face and continue to an open area (bolted lines here - not described). Now head out to the escarpment and the aforementioned routes.

The first three routes are on an isolated pinnacle

❶ Sol y sombra 5
11m. Lovely climbing and position.

❷ Martini bianco 6b
11m. The centre of the face.

❸ Runnel Route 5
12m. Up the crack and runnel.

❹ Desperate Looker . . (7c)
17m. Up the blank shallow arete.

❺ Tequila 7b
17m. A bouldery start to the flake-crack.

❻ Round Head 7a
17m. Harder than it looks to get going.

❼ Little Arete 6c
14m. This one is tucked away right of the gully.

❽ Nicey . . . . 6c+
23m. Climb the bulge to a roof and crack.

❾ Tinto con Limón . . . . . . 7a+
19m. Hard moves direct through the bulge. *Photo on page 5.*

❿ Tinto con Casera . . . . . . 6c+
19m. Move right out of *Tinto con Limón* at the bulge.

⓫ Pacharán con endrinas 6c
22m. An unsatisfying route that tries to climb the arete but fails. *Photo on page 3.*

⓬ Calimocho 6b
13m. Hidden away around the back of the crag behind *Faustino*.

⓭ Licor 6a
13m. Just right of *Calimocho*.

⓮ Faustino . . . . 7b+
14m. Fingery face climbing just to the right of a patch of ivy.

⓯ Moscatel . . . . 6c+
14m. The thin crack to easier ground.

⓰ Pacharán con mier . . . . 7a+
12m. The thin wall just left of a wide corner crack.

⓱ Frexinet . . . . 7a+
15m. The left-hand side of the blunt arete.

Routes 4 to 11

Beer

12
13

14 15 17 18 19 20
16 Hidden in corner

Don Perignon del 69

20m gap

24 25

21 22 23

Next routes 70m

18. **Cruzcampo** . . . . 6a+
15m. The wall and crack on the right-hand side of the blunt arete. *Photo on page 173.*

19 **Don Perignon del 69** . . . 5+
16m. A nice buttress past a mid-height bush.

20 **Widen** . . . . 5+
15m. The wide crack and corner above.

21 **Beer** . . . . 6b+
20m. A thin crack leading to easier climbing above.

22 **Cervezas** . . . . 7a+
20m. A thin crack to a shallow arete in the wall.

23 **Ante la rasca coñac pal cuerpa**
. . . . 6c+
21m. Sustained wall climbing starting left of a block.

24 **Coctel tropical** 6a
10m. The left-hand of two short lines that start high up.

25 **Tómato algo** 6a
10m. The right-hand short line.

26 **Sugumu** . . . . 6c+
25m. A long route up the left-hand side of the wall.

27 **Los niños del rioja** 6c
25m. The central line through the steep mid-height bulge.

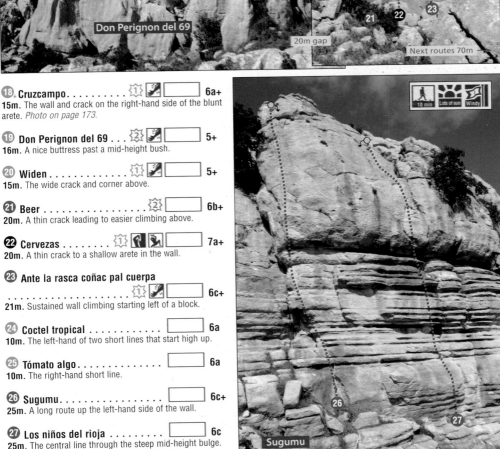

26
27

Sugumu

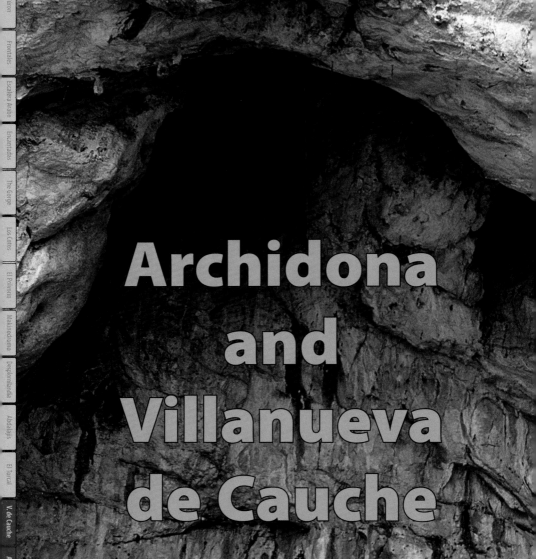

Mijas

Turon

Frontales

Escalera Arabe

Encantados

The Gorge

Los Cotos

El Polvorin

Makinodromo

Desplomilandia

Abdalajis

El Torcal

V. de Cauche

Archidona

Loja

Archidona
and
Villanueva
de Cauche

Rob Sutton working his way across the lip of the main cave at Archidona on the super steep classic *Danza agresiva* (7c) - *page 187*. Photo: Mark Glaister

Mijas

Turon

Frontales

Escalera Arabe

Encantadas

The Gorge

Los Cotos

El Polvorin

Makinodromo

Desplomilandia

Abdalajis

El Torcal

V. de Cauche

Archidona

Loja

'Yugoslavia' is the name given to an eye catching crag close to the small mountain village of Villanueva de Cauche. It is composed of a vertical wall of vivid orange limestone that rises above a grassy slope only seconds from a convenient but quiet road. The crag is also blessed with a southerly, open aspect and a view to die for out over the hills and mountains that run down to the coast and west across to El Torcal. There is a decent spread of grades although the harder lines are the best and all of the climbs are very fingery and technical with progress normally being made on tiny edges and the odd pocket or flake crack. Locating lines on the rather featureless wall is helped by the route names being painted on the rock at the base of the climbs although some of these are now rather tricky to read.

Approach

From El Chorro head for Antequera via Valle de Abdalajis. Go through Antequera following signs for Málaga eventually picking up the A45 motorway. Take this and exit at the Colmenar, Villanueva de Cauche exit. Follow signs for Colmenar (do not go to the village of Villanueva de Cauche) and after 2km the crag is obvious on the left. (1 hour 15 minutes from El Chorro depending on traffic).

Conditions

The crag faces the sun all day but for early risers some shade is possible until mid-morning. The crag is very exposed and is often breezy, it takes no seepage. It might be possible to climb in the rain on the steepest section of the wall.

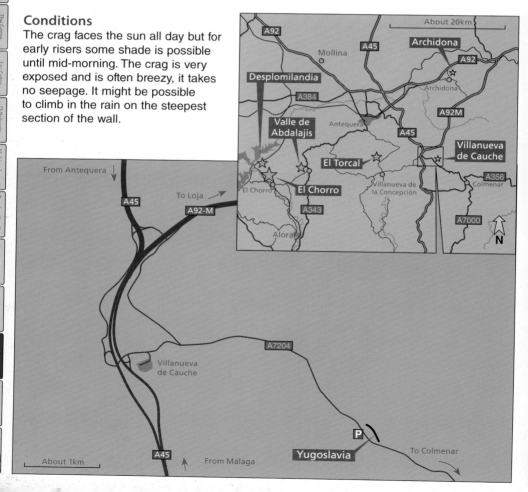

Mijas

Turon

Frontales

Escalera Arabe

Encantadas

The Gorge

Los Cotos

El Polvorin

Makinodromo

Desplomilandia

Abdalajis

El Torcal

V. de Cauche

Archidona

Loja

Mark Glaister on the superb *Diedre candela* (7a+) - *page 183* - at
Villanueva de Cauche. Photo: Lee Proctor (Glaister collection)

Yugoslavia

Yugoslavia is a superbly positioned roadside venue with an enticing orange coloured main face. Many of the routes have their names painted on the rock.

Approach - From the parking pull-out, a number of paths lead up the gentle slope to the base of the cliff. The central section of the crag has a raised ledge from which the harder climbs start.

1 Peluca . . . .   **6a+**
13m. The wall left of a crack in the grey wall at the left end of the crag.

2 ... en escabeche. . . . .   **6a+**
13m. The crack in the grey wall.

3 Salt la tapia . . . .   **6b+**
13m. The arete right of the crack in the grey wall.

4 Er melillero . . . . . .   **6c+**
14m. The pillar with a flake at mid-height.

5 Malozevik **7a**
15m. A good pitch up the shallow curving groove.

6 Al evosia . . . .   **(8b?)**
15m. The blank wall is a project.

7 Chantaje emocional   **(8b?)**
16m. The tall featureless wall looks desperate.

8 Piel palida . . . .   **7c+**
16m. The tough leaning wall left of the pillar.

9 Rascayu **7c**
12m. The short blank wall.

10 Yonky tronky **7b**
9m. The very short blank wall.

11 El frescuni . . . .   **6c+**
18m. A good pitch with a thin hard start.

12 Sin sospecha **7a**
17m. The wall past a flake.

13 Ojos que no ven . . .   **7b**
16m. The very thin wall and overhang above.

14 Los fabulosos manowar   **6c+**
10m. The short thin wall.

15 El lengueton. . . . .   **6b+**
10m. The start of *Diedro Candela* to a lower-off on the left.

16 Finita mix . . . . 🧗🪝 **7a+**
10m/32m. A hard variation start to *Diedro Candela*.

17 Diedre candela . . . . [Top 50] 🪝🔧 **7a+**
32m. The superb groove left of the mid-height overhang.
Photo on page 181.

18 Regional preferente . . . . ☐ **?**
30m. An unfinished line.

19 Vitamin bidon . . . . . ⚙3 🧗🔧 ☐ **7c**
25m. A hard wall climb starting from the left-hand side of the raised ledge.

20 Iron Maiden . . . . ⚙ 🔧 ☐ **8a+**
25m. Start at the gap in the ledge at the base.

21 Poison jimenez . . . . ☐ **?**
32m. A project.

22 Mijya-tovik . . . . ⚙3 🧗🔧🪝 ☐ **8a+**
32m. The smooth sustained wall is very impressive.

23 Supertiri . . . . ⚙3 🪝🧗 ☐ **8a**
32m. Start up a short tufa and slim corner to finish up a thin headwall. Low in the grade.

24 Vas de pro . . . . . . ⚙3 🔧🧗 ☐ **8a**
30m. A very good route. Start just left of the gangway.

25 Diedro 4+1 . . . . ⚙1 🔧 ☐ **5**
25m. The easy-angled left-to-right slanting gangway.

26 Ano mariana . . . . 🪝🧗 ☐ **6c**
10m. The initial wall is very thin.

27 Airbag . . . . 🪝🧗 ☐ **6c**
10m. Similar to *Ano mariana*.

28 El triguevo . . . . ⚙3 🔧 ☐ **6a+**
16m. The slanting groove and orange headwall.

29 Straight Up . . . . ⚙1 ☐ **6a+**
16m. Direct line through *El triguevo*.

30 El biyema . . . . ⚙1 ☐ **6b+**
16m. A direct start tof *El triguevo*.

31 Papa piquillo . . . . ⚙1 🧗 ☐ **6c**
16m. The shallow groove to the upper wall.

32 Gota a gota . . . . . . ⚙1 🧗🔧 ☐ **6b+**
16m. The wall just right of *Papa piquillo.*

33 El milagro de p. tinto . . . . . ⚙1 ☐ **6b**
15m. The broken groove.

34 Moribunda . . . . ☐ **6b+**
13m. A thin wall with a steep start. There is a right-hand branch out of this route which looks to be in the 6b/c range.

35 S'acabo Left . . . . ☐ **(6c)**
13m. The bulges left of a project (known as *S'acabo*).

Lowering-off - Some of these pitches are longer than 30m in length. Take care when lowering off.

2 min | From mid morning

Mijas · Turón · Frontales · Escalera Arabe · Encantadas · The Gorge · Los Cotos · El Polvorin · Makinodromo · Desplomilandia · Abdalajis · El Torcal · V. de Cauche · Archidona · Loja

The main cave of Archidona is one of the World's most impressive sport crags and its line-up of state-of-the-art climbs are worthy of a visit by any climber if only to view just what it is possible to climb. Unfortunately there are no good easier or mid-grade climbs here, even on the margins of the cave, but for climbers looking for good hard routes this is a top spot. The majority of the climbs are extremely long, sustained and overhanging giving spectacular pitches of very high quality. The outlook from the crag is magnificent, the rim of the cave framing the seemingly endless patchwork of olive groves that stretch away to the distant horizon.

Approach

From El Chorro, head for Antequera via Valle de Abdalajis. Go through Antequera following signs for Granada and pick up the main autovia (A92) heading east towards Granada. Follow this to the second Archidona exit (Junction 167). Head towards Archidona and after 0.9km turn left onto a dirt road and then after 0.4km turn left again. 0.6km along this dirt road is the parking (do not block the road). The crag is above you. Follow a path through the olive grove up into the cave. (1 hour 10 minutes from El Chorro depending on traffic).

Conditions

The crag is north facing and receives no sun apart from on its left-hand side late in the day. During the winter it is generally cool but climbable and is a good venue in spring and autumn. Most of the hard routes will be climbable in heavy rain although some of the tufas will begin to seep if it is prolonged.

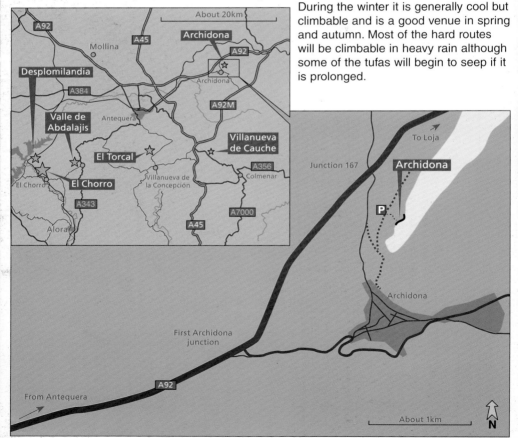

Mijas

Tozo

Frontales

Escalera Arabe

Encantadas

The Gorge

Los Cotos

El Chorro

New Zealand climber Mayan Smith-Gobat on the very steep *Campo amargo* (8a) - *page 187* - at Archidona. Photo: Dave Pickford

Lowering-off - Some of these pitches are longer than 30m in length. Take care when lowering off and use the mid-route lower-offs if necessary.

5 min | Not much sun | Dry in the rain | Seepage

Main Cave

A quite stunning arena that is home to a number of incredibly difficult and daunting routes. Most of the lines are extremely long and sustained and do not see many ascents. This is a good spot in hot weather but does seep after persistent rainfall.

Approach - From the parking pull-in walk up through the olive grove and go through a gate in to the cave.

❶ Amantis religiosa . . . ☆ 🔧 📷 ☐ **7a+**
25m. Start on the far left of the buttress just over the small fence.

❷ Cayo malayo . . . . . ☆ 🔧 📷 ☐ **7a+**
32m. Interesting climbing all the way. A very long pitch.

❸ La canal . . . . ☐ **6a**
20m. The wide cleft which narrows at mid-height.

❹ Posiblmente lluevan piedras
. . . . ☆ 🔧 📷 ☐ **7b+**
26m. A tenuous pitch that follows the right-trending weakness.

❺ Corner Left. . . . . ☆ 🔧 ☐ **7a+**
26m. Climb the line just to the left of the main corner.

❻ Slab Left . . . . ☐ **4+**
20m. Left-hand low angled pitch.

❼ Slab Right . . . . ☐ **4+**
20m. The right-hand low angled pitch.

❽ Rey de azucar . . . . ☐ **8b**
40m. Take a line through the roof and hole high on the left.

❾ Happy Hardcore . . . . ☐ **8c+**
40m. A massive pitch up the continuously steep wall.

❿ Kallisté . . . . . . ☆ 🔧 📷 🔧 ☐ **8c**
40m. The first of a trio of stunning routes. Name at base.

⓫ Salas . . . . ☆ 🔧 📷 ☐ **8b+**
40m. Line through the centre of the mid-height roof.

⓬ Alpechin . . . . . ☆ 🔧 📷 🔧 ☐ **8c**
40m. Climb via tufas up to, and through, the mid-height roof.

⓭ Orujo. . . . . ⌐Top 50⌐ 🔧 📷 🔧 ☐ **9a+**
45m. Start just to the left of the cave and venture out across the lip of the cave and up the leaning headwall. Name at base.

⓮ Piolin . . . . ☐ **8b+**
30m. The line of bolts just right of *Orujo*.

⓯ Primera linea . . . . ☆ 🔧 ☐ **7b+**
25m. The first line on the back wall of the main cave.

Mijas

Turon

Frontales

Escalera Arabe

Encantadas

The Gorge

Los Cotos

El Makinón

16 Lindo gatito .... 🔲🔲 **7b+**
25m. After a bit of a bumble things get a bit more radical!

17 Antonia .... 🔲🔲🔲 **7c**
28m. This one is a bit longer, but no less steep. Spectacular.

18 La penita del perito .... 🔲🔲 **7b**
25m. Start up easy-angled rock to a steep finish.

19 Huele tema .... 🔲 **8a+?**
25m. Move out left from *Campo amargo*.

20 Campo amargo .... 🔲🔲🔲 **8a**
28m. A great trip into upside-down land. Finishing at the first lower-off is **7c+**. *Photo on page 185.*

21 Estado mental .... 🔲🔲 **8c**
40m. A monsterous line across the underside of the cave lip.

22 Transilvania .... 🔲🔲 **8c+**
35m. The line between *Estado mental* and *Danza agresiva*.

23 Danza agresiva ...... Top\L50 🔲 **7c**
30m. A popular classic split by a mid-height cave (**7a+** to here). From the cave, move out left to bring some big tufas to hand. *Photo on page 178.*

24 El precario del sicario .. 🔲🔲 **7c+**
20m. Wildly steep curving line into the midway cave of *Danza agresiva*.

25 Carbunco .... 🔲🔲🔲 **8c**
40m. First of a trio of outrageously sustained climbs.

26 Carbon 14 .... 🔲🔲🔲 **8b+**
40m. The central line.

27 Trance .... 🔲🔲🔲 **8b+**
40m. A superb pitch up the right-hand side of the cave.

28 Gurú .... 🔲🔲 **6b+**
20m. Left-hand line up wall just outside of the fence.

29 Demolition Man .... 🔲🔲 **6c**
20m. The right-hand line up the steep wall just outside fence.

Loja

Mijas

Turon

Frontales

Escalera Arabe

Encantadas

Tin Gorge

Los Frias

El Polvorin

Phil Black working his way up the twin tufa pipes of *Hasta luego Luca* (7b) - *page 197* - one of many fabulous lines at Loja. Photo: Mark Glaister

Loja | Archidona | V. de Cauche | El Torcal | Abdalajís | Desplomilandia | Maximdromo | El Polvorín | Los Cotos | The Gorge | Encantadas | Escalera Árabe | Frontales | Turón | Mijas

The high and shady crags of Loja are located way above a picturesque landscape of sprawling olive plantations and distant mountain ranges. The climbing is exceptional with route after route offering steep and sustained wall climbing, more often than not on tufas and pockets. There is plenty of climbing for those operating from grade 6 upwards and a number of the routes are surprisingly long but most are single pitches.

Loja is around one and a half hours drive from El Chorro but is well worth the effort as the drive itself is interesting. The cliff is easily accessed, and on warm days the climbing is superb. In the past there has been a bird restriction but this has now been lifted. The area has now also been designated as a National Park.

Approach

From El Chorro, head for Antequera by following the road through Valle de Abdalajis. Go through Antequera, following signs for Granada, and pick up the main road (A92) heading east towards Granada. Follow this as far as the first exit signed for the town of Loja (junction 187) but continue just beyond and turn off to a large service area. Drive to the start of the entry sliproad back on to the main road and turn right on to a good dirt track that runs parallel to the road. Follow the track to some buildings and turn right uphill and follow the track for 2.5km until Zorreras Altas is easily seen on the left close to the top of the mountain. Park at the side of the track taking great care to leave plenty of space for large quarry lorries to pass. Zorreras Altas is just above the track and Zorreras Bajas is easily accessed by a contouring path that starts at a gate/gap in the fence on the right-hand side of the track.

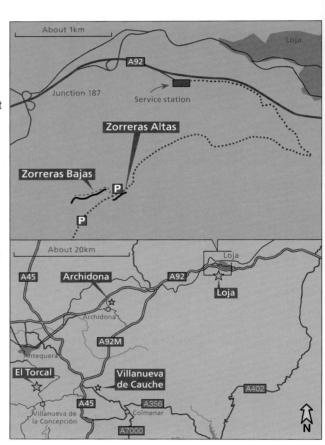

Conditions

The crags are at an altitude of 1000m and remain in the shade for most of the day, being a haven of cool when the temperatures at lower levels are unpleasantly high. It is a particularly useful crag for the visitor in early autumn or late spring. Climbing would be possible if it starts to rain but it is not really somewhere to go looking for dry rock in prolonged rain.

There are other crags in the Loja area, but general they are not as good as this one. They lend to be at a lower altitude and face the sun so might be worth a look in winter.

A climber approaches the upper moves of the brilliant wall climb *Patranas* (6a+) - *page 193* - high above the olive plantations below Loja. Photo: Mark Glaister

- *page 193* -

Mijas

Turon

Frontales

Escalera Arabe

Encantadas

The Gorge

Los Cotos

El Polvorin

Makinodromo

Desplomilandia

Abdalajís

El Torcal

V. de Cauche

Archidona

Loja

Zorreras Altas

A long low wall of good rock perched just above the approach track. There are some lovely steep wall climbs and a few tufa pipes that add some variety. The majority of the better climbs are in the mid grades. There is no sun to be had here and the crag is very exposed to the wind with no shelter, but in warm weather the conditions will be perfect.

Approach - The crag is above the road just before it reaches the top of the hill.

1 Canibales a dieta . . . . . 7a+
17m. The thin grey tufa is low in the grade.

2 Arakatak . . . . (8?)
20m. The wall right of the thin tufa is hard.

Esinifando rojas

Roadside | Not much sun | Windy

3 Numeros rojos . . . . 7b+
20m. The fine central line.

4 Esinifando rojas 7b
20m. The pale-coloured wall just left of the diagonal crack.

5 Un espiritu zoquete 6c
20m. The diagonal crack is gained via the short wall.

6 Treprorzas . . . . 5+
20m. Right of some broken ground is a striking left-to-right line.

7 Danza prima . . . . . 6a+
18m. Start behind the large boulder and follow the thin cracks to finish as for *Treprorzas*.

8 Buraka . . . . 6a+
22m. The left-hand line up the bulging wall to a high lower off.

9 Cepillos free . . . . 6a+
22m. The right-hand of two close lines.

10 Exculibiertu . . . . 5+
22m. Good sustained climbing. The first bolt is high.

11 Bongui boy 6c
15m. A tight eliminate up the blank wall.

12 Hoito con el hito 6c
15m. Another very thin wall climb.

13 Nirvana 6b
19m. Long line moving rightwards to a lower-off.

14 Domino paria 6c
19m. The central line on this section of wall.

15 Aprenaiz de fakir . . . . 6c+
19m. The thin right-hand line.

Roadside | Not much sun | Windy

Nirvana

Next routes adjoining

Patranas

16 Albergue de emplumados
.... 7b+
20m. Take the grey and cream streaked overhanging wall.

17 Ukachaka........ 7c
20m. The steep wall and bulge.

18 Pretensiones 7b
20m. The good wall and shallow upper groove.

19 Perros de presa 8a
20m. The perfectly formed top-to-toe tufa. May be only 7c+.

20 Sangre fria............. (7b+)
19m. The good looking short tufa leads to the wall above.

21 Yukatan........... 7b+
18m. The wall past an orange hole.

22 Los druidas 7b
18m. The wall and short orange streak.

23 Hasta los guevos .... 7b+
18m. Climb the thin grey streak.

24 Perchomania .... 7a+
18m. A less attractive wall.

25 ? .... ?
18m. The short left-facing corner and wall is bolted but no details are known.

26 Vicio de vacio .... 6c+
20m. The left-hand line up the thin white wall.

27 D'lulu 6c
20m. A good pitch that has some fingery moves around the overlap high up.

28 Patranas .... 6a+
20m. A fine steep pitch on spaced pockets. *Photo on page 191.*

29 Sidroterapia ...... 6b+
20m. The harder but equally worthwhile line out of *Patranas*.

30 D'ayo 6b
20m. The right-hand line on the white wall.

31 Penumbra 7b
19m. Steep wall just right of easy broken ground.

32 Iven, devorame!........ 8a
19m. The thin wall past a tiny mid-height bulge.

33 Mostacho blanco 7a
19m. A good pitch past a small hole.

34 Karkatrepos .... 6c+
19m. A good but tough wall route.

35 Rosky 6b
20m. Tackle the left side of the low cave and wall above.

36 Sir Lancelot .... 6c+
20m. Good but powerful climbing out of the low cave.

37 Aracadia 6b
20m. An excellent pitch up the very right-hand side of the wall.

38 D'brokers............. 6b
17m. A poor pitch around to the right of the main crag.

Mijas
Turon
Frontales
Escalera Arabe
Encantadas
The Gorge
Los Cotos
El Polvorin
Makinodromo
Desplomilandia
Abdalajis
El Torcal
V de Gaucin
Archidona
Loja

Zorreras Bajas - Left

The lower walls at Loja present a series of excellent buttresses and steep walls. The grades tend to be in the mid and upper ranges and you probably need to be leading at least 6c to begin to appreciate the place.
Approach - From the parking areas, locate the rough gate in the fence on the downhill side of the road, just below the start of the Zorreras Altas section of crag. Go through the gate and follow a path that descends slightly until the crag comes into sight.

The first section of crag reached is easily identified by the large, ground-level cave in its centre. Although not huge, the routes are sustained and strenuous and give some shelter in poor weather. The rock is excellent.

❶ Eguzilore . . . . 🔲🔲 **6c**
16m. The farthest left line past tufas is a good pitch.

❷ Genio y figura . . . . 🔲🔲 **6c+**
16m. Great moves up tufa to a wide groove.

❸ Teta capochina . . . . 🔲 **8a**
16m. The thin wall and rib above a tufa trunk.

❹ Deltoya . . . . 🔲🔲🔲 **7b**
17m. A tufa fin to a blank grey sheet.

❺ Musho . . . . 🔲🔲🔲 **7b+**
17m. Tufa pipes to a steep headwall.

❻ Colrin Colorado . . . . . . 🔲🔲 **8a**
17m. The steep left edge of the cave to a rib left of some vegetation.

There are a couple of projects in the depths of the cave.

❼ Idioma Galveciano . 🔲🔲🔲 **7b+**
17m. A curving line around the right rim of the cave.

20m to the right is another less attractive section of the crag that nevertheless has a number of interesting lines on its left side. Some of the rock on the right-hand side of the wall is friable.

❽ La malicia del enano . . 🔲🔲 **7b**
17m. The slightly broken line on the left-hand side of sector.

❾ Atila matatino . . . . 🔲🔲 **7b**
17m. The steep and unrelenting tufa and pockets

❿ Zingaros . . . . 🔲🔲 **7a**
17m. The steep orange wall on pockets is worthwhile.

⓫ Energia renovable . . . . . 🔲🔲 **7c+**
18m. A good lower wall to hard tufas on a high rib.

⓬ De Sopeton . . . . 🔲🔲 **7b**
18m. An easy but broken lower wall to an overhanging finish.

⓭ Tragos amargos . . . . . . 🔲🔲 **7b+**
18m. The gradually-steepening line on orange rock.

⓮ Tirar a matar . . . . 🔲 **(7c?)**
18m. A very steep line up odd-looking orange rock.

Projects

Deltoya

Next routes - 20m

The next routes are on a compact wall of great rock that has a some good pitches and one very worthwhile 6c.

15 Chut chut **6b**
14m. The left-hand side of the high orange wall above a slab.

16 La terrible **6b**
14m. The right-hand line above the slab.

17 Avistamiento **6c**
13m. The short thin wall starting up a corner.

18 Gorgolas **6c**
17m. Brilliant climbing up the left side of the pillar.

19 Karadura **7a**
17m. A harder companion to *Gorgolas*.

20 Mortal up . . . . **6c+**
17m. Some interesting but unbalanced moves.

21 Corazon amigo **6c**
17m. The left-trending line to a steep finish.

Gorgolas

Zorreras Bajas Right - 50m

Zingaros

Route 15 to 21 - 60m

Mijas
Túron
Frontales
Escalera Árabe
Encantadas
The Gorge
Los Cotos
El Polvorín
Makinodromo
Desplomilandia
Abdalajís
El Torcal
V. de Cauche
Archidona

Osos can

From Bajas Left - 50m

Bolts

Sidebar tabs (left margin): Mijas · Turon · Frontales · Escalera árabe · Encantadas · The Gorge · Los Cotos · El Polvorín · Maklinodromo · Desplomilandia · Abdalajís · El Torcal · V de Cuarzo · Archidona · Loja

Zorreras Bajas - Right

An impressive bulging wall of pocketed and tufa-strewn rock that has some difficult and powerful lines. Some of the routes on the right have glued-on holds. Recent developments have extended some of the lines and a few new pitches have been added on the left which has made the lines hard to distinguish, however the names of the routes are painted on the rock.

1 Tapas **7c**
15m. The cream-coloured wall via a right-trending pocket line.

2 Sa acabo Norma . . . . **7c+**
13m. A vicious and steep line on pockets.

3 San Miguel **8a**
13m. The line of tufa blobs and holes. Low in the grade.

4 Oficina punk . . . . **7b+**
13m. The bulging wall on finger pockets.

5 La cima del mundo . . . . **8a+**
14m. A tendon-tweaker up the bulging wall on tiny finger pockets.

6 Desesperado . . . . **8a+**
15m. A tufa to bulging pocketed wall.

7 Osos can **8a**
15m. Steep contorted tufas lead to the upper wall.

8 Como gato panzamba . . **7c**
15m. A tufa and wall right of contorted tufas of *Osos can*.

9 Tarari que te vi **7c**
15m. The blank cream wall to an overhanging finish.

10 De espaldus el mundo . . **7b+**
16m. The wall and upper bulge are low in the grade.

11 Al abordaja **7b**
16m. The lower wall to a powerful finish through the top overhangs.

12 A la deriva . . . . **7b+**
16m. A very strange set of glued-on pebble holds.

13 A lo mierda **7a**
16m. The easiest line on the wall builds to a steep finish.

14 El temazo . . . . **7c+**
16m. A very hard pitch on the right-hand side of the wall.

15 La zorra y las chapas . . . . . **7a+**
1) 7a+, 15m. A thin technical line running rightwards to a belay.
2) 6a+, 16m. Move right to a line of bolts and climb to belay.
3) 7a+, 8m. Short steep pitch to the top. Abseil or walk off.

16 Violacion de monaguillos **7c+**
10m. A short steep line rising from the small alcove.

17 Goco . . . . **7c+**
13m. A hard pitch climbing up the right side of the alcove. Above are more bolts but the grade is not known.

⑱ El tratante . . . . ⟨2⟩ ☐ 8b
1) 5+, 10m. A short easy first pitch gains a ledge and belay.
2) 8b, 25m. Above is a long hard pitch.
3) ?, 9m. A short steep finish for which the grade is not known.

⑲ Conclave . . . . ☐ 5
10m. A short pitch to a ledge, above which bolts are in place but details are not known.

⑳ Oye Brother . . . . ☐ 5+
10m. Another short pitch to the ledge, above which bolts are in place but details are not known.

㉑ La malafolla . . . . ⟨3⟩ 🪝 ☐ 8b
27m. The line just left of the ledge at 10m.

㉒ Morituring . . . . ⟨2⟩ ☐ 8b
27m. The line just right of *La malafolla*.

㉓ Murcianicos . . . . ⟨3⟩ 🪝 ☐ 8b
27m. A stupendous line up the left wall of the depression.

㉔ Desvariante de levante . ⟨3⟩ 🪝 ☐ 8c
35m. Move right out of *Murcianicos*.

㉕ La sombra de cain . . . . ⟨3⟩ 🪝 ☐ 8a+
35m. Tufa and pockets from the hole in the back of the alcove.

㉖ De poder a poder . . . . . ⟨3⟩ 🪝 ☐ 8a+
27m. A thin tufa and wall rising from the back of the alcove.

㉗ Voraz . . . . ⟨3⟩ 🪝 ☐ 8a
27m. The stunning line up the back of the alcove.

㉘ Vibraciones positivas . . ⟨3⟩ 🪝 ☐ 8a
35m. Yet another awesome line

㉙ El terror de los germenes . . ⟨1⟩ ☐ 8a
35m. Start up the rib right of the steep alcove.

㉚ Morada de vampiros . . . ⟨2⟩ 🪝 ☐ 7a+
30m. Good climbing to a lower-off in the high cave.

㉛ La rambla del mago . . . . . . ⟨1⟩ ☐ 7b
17m. Climb to overhang. It may have been extended at **7b+**.

㉜ La palide . . . . ⟨3⟩ 🪝 🪝 ☐ 8a+
35m. The wall past three horizontal holes at 12m.

㉝ Dos itanos . . . . ⟨3⟩ 🪝 ☐ 7b+
21m. The beautiful tufa to a mid-height lower-off. The continuation is unknown. *Photo on page 199.*

㉞ Hasta luego Luca . . . . . ⟨Top 50⟩ 🪝 ☐ 7b
21m. Classic twin tufas to a lower-off. The extension is **8a**.
Photos on page 38 and 188.

[Icons: 5 min / Not much sun / Windy / Seepage / Dry in the rain]

Lowering-off - Some of these pitches are longer than 30m in length. Take care when lowering off.

Bolts | 18 19 20 21 22 23 25 26 27 28 29 30 31 32 33 34

Voraz

Zorreras Bajas - Far Right

Another great section of crag that is fairly popular. Some of the lines have now been extended and this has reduced the number of easier lines.

1 La perversa ...... 🔲 8a
32m. An awesome line heading for the left-hand side of the thin grey tufa high on the crag, just right of *Hasta luego Luca*.

2 Todo es mentirra .. 🔲 8a
32m. Grey streaks up the blank wall.

3 Aliento del dragon . 🔲 8a
32m. A thin wall to a blank upper section.

4 Vida indecente .... 🔲 7c+
32m. The impressive wall and tufa.

The next three climbs all used to have a mid-height lower-off but have now been rebolted and extended to the top of the crag and the lower belay has gone. They are all now considerably harder than they used to be.

5 Tela marinera........ 🔲 7c
30m. A pleasant first half gains twin tufas that are climbed to the final steep wall.

Lowering-off - Some of these pitches are longer than 30m in length. Take care when lowering off.

6 Enrezabia .... 🔲 7b+
30m. A hard upper half that finishes via some powerful lock-offs on the final section up the headwall.

7 Panceta............ 🔲 7b
30m. Take the nice wall just to the left of a rib to tufas and the bulging headwall.

8 A sombrao............. 🔲 7b+
30m. Climb out of the alcove and continue up gradually steepening ground to the top. Low in the grade.

9 Piperra .... 🔲 6c+
28m. Fine climbing on pockets all the way to the top.

10 Puta navidad ..... 🔲 6c
26m. A really nice climb with a slightly powerful pull at the final bulge.

11 Helao recalentao ..... 🔲 6c+
26m. Good sustained wall climbing to a bulge at the top.

12 Diagnostico precoz .... 🔲 7a
26m. The grey streak to a light-coloured bulge.

13 Polvoreda .... 🔲 7a
26m. Thin wall climbing at the far right-hand end of the crag.

5 min | Not much sun | Windy | Seepage

Frontales

Escalera Arabe

Encantadas

The Gorge

Los Cotos

El Polvorin

Makinodromo

Desplomilandia

Abdalajis

El Torcal

V. de Cauche

Archidona

Loja

Mark Glaister redpoints the superbly sustained tufa climb *Dos itanos* (7b+) - *page 197* - at Loja. Photo: Glaister Collection.

Abdalajis	162	Las Encantadas	96
Archidona	184	Loja	188
Cotos	120	Los Cotos	120
Desplomilandia	148	Makinodromo	136
El Chorro	62	Mijas	44
El Polvorin	130	Polvorin	130
El Torcal	170	Torcal	170
Encantadas	96	Túron	52
Escalera Arabe	82	Valle de Abdalajis	162
Frontales	62	Villanueva de Cauche	178
Gorge, The	104	Yugoslavia	178

Access	8	Flights	20	Roads	22
Accommodation	28	Gear	32	Rockfax Guides	Back flap
Acknowledgements	14	Gorge Approaches	108	Rockfax Route Database	8
Advertiser Directory	16	Grade Colour-codes	33	Ropes	32
Bulls	26	Graded List	38	Route Names	7
Camino del Rey	107	Grades	33	Route Symbols	Front Flap
Camping	28	Guidebook History	7	Shops	26
Car Hire	20	Introduction	4	Symbols Key	Front Flap
Climbing Shops	26	Makinodromo Approach	138	Top 50	38
Conditions Planner	Back Flap	Map Key	Front Flap	Topo Key	Front Flap
Contents	3	Other Guides	36	Travel Insurance	26
Crag Symbols	Front Flap	Public Holidays	24	Upper Gorge	8
Crag Table	42	Public Transport	22	Walkway	107
Deutsch (Einleitung)	12	Rack	32	Weather	24
Español (Introducción)	10	Railway Tunnels	8, 109	When to Go	24
Feedback	8	Refuges	28	Without a Car	20

Mountain Rescue

Dial 112 - Ensure you have details of your location and what the incident involves. This number works on any mobile on a Spanish network.